Tennessee Williams

Mitchell Lane
PUBLISHERS

P.O. Box 196
Hockessin, Delaware 19707

Poets and Playwrights

Carl Sandburg

Emily Dickinson

Langston Hughes

Tennessee Williams

William Shakespeare

Tennessee Williams

Kathleen Tracy

Copyright © 2007 by Mitchell Lane Publishers, Inc. All rights reserved. No part of this book may be reproduced without written permission from the publisher. Printed and bound in the United States of America.

Printing   1   2   3   4   5   6   7   8   9

Library of Congress Cataloging-in-Publication Data
Tracy, Kathleen.
   Tennessee Williams / by Kathleen Tracy.
      p. cm. — (Poets and playwrights)
   Includes bibliographical references and index.
   ISBN 1-58415-427-6 (lib. bdg.)
1. Williams, Tennessee, 1911–1983—Juvenile literature. 2. Dramatists, American—20th century—Biography—Juvenile literature. I. Title. II. Series.
PS3545.I5365Z854 2006
812'.54—dc22

2006006106

ISBN: 9781584154273

ABOUT THE AUTHOR: Kathleen Tracy has been a journalist for over twenty years. Her writing has been featured in magazines including *The Toronto Star*'s "Star Week," *A&E Biography* magazine, *KidScreen* and *Variety*. She is also the author of numerous biographies and other nonfiction books, including *Mariano Guadalupe Vallejo, William Hewlett: Pioneer of the Computer Age, The Watergate Scandal, The Life and Times of Cicero, Mariah Carey, Kelly Clarkson,* and *The Plymouth Colony: The Pilgrims Settle in New England* for Mitchell Lane Publishers. She divides her time between homes in Studio City and Palm Springs, California.

PHOTO CREDITS: Cover, pp. 1, 3, 56—Ann Rosener/Pix Inc./Getty Images; p. 6—George Karger/Pix Inc./Time Life Pictures/Getty Images; pp. 16, 66—Library of Congress; pp. 26, 36—Associated Press; p. 30—Bettman/Corbis; p. 46—Eileen Darby/Time Life Pictures/Getty Images; p. 74—Getty Images; p. 82—New York Times Co./Getty Images; p. 90—William E. Sauro/New York Times Co./Getty Images.

PUBLISHER'S NOTE: This story is based on the author's extensive research, which she believes to be accurate. Documentation of such research is contained on pages 107–109.
   The internet sites referenced herein were active as of the publication date. Due to the fleeting nature of some web sites, we cannot guarantee they will all be active when you are reading this book.

PLB

Contents

*For Your Information

Julie Haydon and Anthony Ross costarred as Laura and the Gentleman Caller in the original Broadway production of *The Glass Menagerie*. After a disastrous preview in Chicago, the producer nearly shut the production down before its scheduled New York run. The play was saved by the glowing reviews of theater critic Claudia Cassidy, and *The Glass Menagerie* made its Broadway debut on March 31, 1945.

Chapter 1

An Overnight Success

It was only a week before Christmas in 1944, but Tennessee Williams felt no holiday cheer. A winter storm was pummeling the city and the cold, blustery weather outside matched his bleak mood. He was in Chicago at the Civic Theater, where his play *The Glass Menagerie* was in the final days of rehearsal before its pre-Broadway opening in the Windy City. The rehearsal was not going well.

At thirty-three, Williams had hoped this would be the big theater break he'd been waiting for to finally redeem his career. His first produced play, *Battle of Angels,* had opened in Boston almost four years to the day earlier and had been a complete disaster. Audiences booed and the producers came on stage to personally apologize. The play closed after just two weeks, never making it to Broadway. Williams had waited years for this second chance, and now it all seemed to be slipping away again.

The production had started out so promising. Williams's agent, Audrey Wood, sent the play to Eddie Dowling, a producer-director-actor who agreed to produce *Menagerie* because he wanted to play Tom, the male protagonist. Williams was thrilled—even though Dowling was forty-nine and the character of Tom was supposed to be in his early thirties.

Nor did Williams care that Dowling's financial backer was a mysterious—and probably shady—Chicago businessman. Mr. Louis Singer had become rich by operating a number of rundown, fleabag hotels.

The Glass Menagerie, which is often referred to as a memory play, is intensely autobiographical. It tells the story of the Wingfields—an aging mother, Amanda, who spends much of her time daydreaming about the past; Laura, an emotionally fragile and physically impaired daughter who avoids reality by obsessing over her collection of glass animal figurines; and Tom, the disenchanted son who knows he needs to escape and find his own way in the world.

"Memory takes a lot of poetic license," Tom says in the first scene. "It omits some details; others are exaggerated according to the emotional value of the articles it touches, for memory is seated predominantly in the heart. . . . I give you truth in the pleasant disguise of illusion."[1]

Casting was left to Dowling, and for the role of the matriarch Amanda, he convinced well-known stage actress Laurette Taylor to come out of retirement. It was a bold—some said suicidal—casting choice. Nobody could question Taylor's acting ability . . . when she was sober. After the death of her husband many years earlier, she had sunk into depression and alcoholism and had spent many years living reclusively. Now sixty, it was a chance for Taylor to make a triumphant comeback in the Broadway-bound play.

In the days before opening night, Williams doubted the show would make it past the first week. Although she brought just the right pathos to the role, Taylor seemed incapable of memorizing her lines. That she frequently appeared in danger of falling over in a drunken stupor didn't inspire confidence, either.

Williams would later recall his dismay watching her in rehearsals. The dialogue she did know "she was still delivering in a Southern accent which she had acquired from some long-ago black domestic. . . . I was sitting in a corner wondering what menial occupation was next in store for me."[2]

It wasn't just Taylor's lack of focus that burdened Williams's play. The theater's cheap sound system was tinny, the backer had not given them any money for publicity, the theater was located away from Chicago's main theater district, and the snowstorm threatened to keep audiences home for opening night.

When Mr. Singer stopped by to see how rehearsals were going, he was so appalled, the rehearsal was canceled. Dowling went out later with theater critic George Jean Nathan and the two discussed what could be done to salvage the production. As it happened, the two men also got riotously drunk and in their state of inebriation decided what the play needed: a scene in which Tom gets drunk!

To keep the peace, and to get rehearsals back on track, codirector Margo Jones and Williams agreed to add the scene—where it remains to this day.

What nobody realized until the play's first preview performance was that there was sheer genius to Laurette's Taylor's apparent madness. "You see," Williams later explained, "Laurette knew she didn't have to give her lines until the play opened, so she was watching the others, observing, waiting. But at the time we didn't know that. I thought she didn't know her lines and so did everybody else."[3]

They invited the cast of another play appearing in Chicago to see a preview, "and that's when we discovered what Laurette had been up to. This lady knew every line—and then some. . . . She was a great, great person."[4]

Even so, the rest of the production was chaotic. An insecure Dowling kept asking Williams for rewrites and the staging had actors bumping into one another. The frustrated playwright pointedly told Dowling, "Art is experience remembered in tranquility. And I find no tranquility in Chicago."[5]

On December 26, 1944, *The Glass Menagerie* opened. Minutes before the curtain rose, it seemed everyone's worst fears had materialized. Nobody could find Laurette. However, the panicked crew breathed relief when they found her in the bathroom trying on a robe she had to wear later in the play and wondering why everyone was so stressed.

The actors performed before a half-empty theater of attendees unaware they were witnessing history. The play didn't follow a traditional theatrical structure—Tom spoke directly to the audience as he narrated his "memories"—and the play was full of lyrical imagery. Many left unsure what exactly they had seen.

Williams was aware he had challenged his audience, perhaps too much. "In Chicago the first night, no one knew how to take *Menagerie*. It was something of an innovation in the theater and even though Laurette gave an incredibly luminous, electrifying performance and people observed it. But people are people, and most of them went home afterward to take at least equal pleasure in their usual entertainments."[6]

The next afternoon, Mr. Singer announced the show would close—but there had been two people in the audience who would make sure that wouldn't happen. Chicago theater critics Claudia Cassidy, who wrote for the *Chicago Daily Tribune,* and *Herald-American*'s Ashton Stevens gave the play enthusiastic reviews.

Cassidy wrote, "Too many theatrical bubbles burst in the blowing, but *The Glass Menagerie* holds in its shadowed fragility the stamina of success. . . .

"Tennessee Williams, who wrote the play, has been incredibly lucky. His play, which might have been smashed by the insensitive or botched by the fatuous, has fallen into expert hands . . . ah, that Laurette Taylor!" She summed up by saying, "If it is your play, as it is mine, it reaches out . . . and you are caught in its spell."[7]

Stevens was equally smitten, observing the play had "the courage of true poetry couched in colloquial prose."[8]

Despite their glowing reviews, attendance remained challenged for the next week. "It took that lovely lady, Claudia Cassidy," Williams recounted, "a lot of time to sell it to them, to tell them it was special."[9]

The first reviews were enough to convince Mr. Singer to remove the closing notice. Even though Mayor Edward Kelly agreed to have the city pay half the ticket price for municipal workers who attended a performance, ticket sales remained sluggish going into the new year. Cassidy attended more performances and continued urging her readers to go see the play.

"I never heard of [Tennessee Williams] . . . until Eddie Dowling wrote me about *The Glass Menagerie.* I haven't a notion what he looks like or how he sounds when he talks. But when he writes he speaks the theatre's language and his play reached out to me. . . . . It is deeply etched as a sudden stab of memory, as poignant in detail as a dream . . . some of its dialogue haunts you. . . . Things like this remind you sharply how much of your life you spend in the dreary treadmill of inertia that is the theater's second best. It's harder to accept the shoddy substitute after your eyes and ears have had such rich reminder of the real thing. . . .

"I saw it three times in three days and will be going back, which is risky business in the realm of make believe. But it is an honest, tender, tough, and, to me, brilliant play."[10]

Her persistence finally started to pay dividends. In the middle of January, she reported in her theater column: "Good news over the week-end was that box office receipts doubled for *The Glass Menagerie* from the week before, a cheering circumstance to those who cherish the play and hope it sticks in Chicago, for all Broadway's hopeful angling."[11]

By the end of the month, the actors began playing to standing-room-only houses. In her reviews, Cassidy had continued to single out Taylor's Amanda, and it was clear to Williams that Laurette—even though she continued to drink heavily—was carving out a masterful performance.

"Actually, she directed many of the scenes, particularly the ones between mother and daughter, and she did a top-notch job," reported Donald Spoto. "She was continually working on her part, putting in little things and taking them out—almost every night in Chicago there was something new—but she never disturbed the central characterization. Everything she did was absolutely in character."[12]

News of Taylor's star turn and the buzz surrounding the play prompted many people to fly in from New York to see whether the hype was justified. Convinced that it was, even before *Menagerie* opened in New York, it was *the* play to see. Ironically, Dowling had yet to even secure a theater for the play.

Finally, it was time to move the play to Broadway. On March 31, 1945, *The Glass Menagerie* premiered at the Playhouse Theatre to a packed house crackling with anticipation. Joining Dowling and Taylor were their costars from Chicago—Julie Haydon as Laura and Anthony Ross, who played Laura's gentleman caller.

The response to the play was staggering. The audience rose in unison to give the cast a standing ovation and kept cheering and applauding through an unheard-of twenty-five curtain calls. They urged the playwright to take a bow, which he finally—and reluctantly—did.

"I was sitting in the fourth row and somebody extended a hand to me and I went up on the stage," he recalled in his memoirs. "And I felt embarrassed; I don't think I felt any great sense of triumph. I think writing is continually a pursuit of a very elusive quarry, and you never quite catch it."[13]

Just five days earlier Tennessee had celebrated his thirty-fourth birthday. And with one performance, he was suddenly being hailed as one of the American theater's most important voices. Two weeks later, *The Glass Menagerie* was awarded the New York Drama Critics' Circle Award for Best American Play of the Year. The play would run for 563 performances, until August 3, 1946.

Ironically, success would prove an uncomfortable fit for the playwright, who would later observe, "Once you fully apprehend the vacuity of a life without struggle, you are equipped with the basic means of salvation."[14]

For better or worse, *The Glass Menagerie* would change Williams' life forever. It would also revolutionize American theater.

"It is usually forgotten what a revolution his first great success meant to the New York theater," Arthur Miller would write. "*The Glass Menagerie* in one stroke lifted lyricism to its highest level in our theater's history, but it broke new ground in another way. What was new in Tennessee Williams was his rhapsodic insistence that form serve his utterance rather than dominating the cramping it. In him, the American theater found, perhaps for the first time, an eloquence and amplitude of feeling. And driving on this newly discovered lyrical line was a kind of emotional heroism; he wanted not to approve or disapprove but to touch the germ of life and to celebrate it with verbal beauty."[15]

It is usually said that the best writing comes from what we know. Most of Williams's work resonates with familiarity and a kinship with the flawed characters that populate his worlds. He was a restless spirit in search of himself. Like Tom Wingfield, he was never able to completely shed the ghosts of his childhood, which both haunted him and laid the foundation for one of the greatest careers of letters the world has ever seen.

Laurette Taylor

Laurette Taylor

During her time, Laurette Taylor was considered one of the most accomplished stage actresses in modern American theater. Even so, the drama and intrigue of her life off-stage often overshadowed—and hindered—her prodigious talent.

She was born Helen Loretta Cooney on April Fools' Day in 1884. Her desire to perform was a source of friction between her parents—her mother dreamed of stardom for her daughter while her father thought life in the theater was unseemly. He was outnumbered. When Laurette was twelve, she made her stage debut at a vaudeville theater in Lynn, Massachusetts, using the name La Belle Laurette.

Three years later she was cast by playwright Charles Taylor in the touring company production of *King of the Opium Ring*. Even though he was twenty years older, in 1901 they married. They had two children, Dwight and Marguerite.

Over the next six years, Laurette appeared in several more of his plays, including her Manhattan debut in *From Rags to Riches*. Unfortunately, the marriage didn't work as well as their professional collaboration, and in 1910, the couple split.

Laurette's lifelong dream of performing on Broadway was finally realized in May 1909 when she appeared in J. Hartley Manners's *The Great John Ganton* at the Lyric Theatre on Forty-Second Street. She married Manners in 1912, who had written *Peg o' My Heart* for her. That play would make Laurette a star.

In the play, Taylor played a young Irish woman sent off to relatives in Britain who are charged with making her a proper lady. After a preview run in Los Angeles, the comedy opened at New York's Cort Theatre in December 1912. Although critical response was indifferent, audiences fell in love with Taylor and the show would ultimately run for a then-record of 604 performances. The play was also a global hit, and by 1919, Manners had earned more than $1 million in royalties—the equivalent of more than 10 million in today's dollars.

Taylor was at the peak of her career. She and Manners were the toast of Broadway, and their home was always full of famous writers and actors. Noel Coward used them as the inspiration for his comedy *Hay Fever*. But the good times would come to an abrupt and tragic end.

A week before Christmas in 1928, Manners died. Over the previous few years the marriage had been troubled, prompting Laurette to start drinking excessively. Manners's death sent her on a decade-long binge, and despite an occasional performance here and there, she became such a recluse that even some former friends assumed she was dead.

By the time Eddie Dowling tracked her down, she was living in a hotel. In exchange for free acting lessons, an aspiring young actress named Eloise Sheldon took care of Laurette and became a devoted companion. She recalled to David Spoto the day the script for *The Glass Menagerie* was delivered: "Of course, her first reaction was to turn it down," Sheldon said. "She thought her career was over."[16]

Encouraged by Eloise and her daughter Marguerite, Taylor finally accepted, and her turn as Amanda Wingfield would become the stuff of Broadway legend. At sixty years old, she was once again the toast of Broadway. It would be a bittersweet comeback.

While most assumed Taylor's frequent vomiting offstage during performances was caused either by nerves or by the effects of too much alcohol, the truth was more sobering—she had developed cancer. Despite her advancing illness, she never missed a performance. On December 7, 1946, four months after her final performance of *The Glass Menagerie*, Laurette died of a heart attack. She was just sixty-two years old.

Tennessee Williams was staying in New Orleans working on what would eventually become *A Streetcar Named Desire* when he learned of Taylor's passing. Three years later, he wrote a remembrance of her for the *New York Times*:

> I consider her the greatest artist of her profession that I have known . . . there was a radiance about her art which I can compare only to the greatest lines of poetry. I loved her as a person. In a way the second is more remarkable . . . because I have always been so awkward and diffident around actors that it has made a barrier between us almost all but insuperable.
>
> In the case of Laurette Taylor, I cannot say that I ever got over the awkwardness and the awe which originally were present, but she would not allow it to stand between us. The great warmth of her heart burned through and we became close friends. I am afraid it is the only close friendship I have ever had with a player.[17]

Williams described her courage in working through the pain of her illness. "She was neither a well nor strong person at any time during the run of the play and often continued her performance when a person of ordinary spirit would not have dared to. Even when throat trouble made it painful for her to speak she continued in her demanding part and I have never seen her physical suffering affect the unfailing wonder of her performance. . . . She remained in the part that long because of a heroic perseverance I find as magnificent as her art itself."[18]

After her death, a collection of Taylor's letters and other documents were donated to the University of Texas at Austin. The collection is available to the public for viewing.

The MIKADO

POOH BAH.

The Mikado is one of Gilbert and Sullivan's most famous collaborations. The operetta tells the story of Prince Nanki-Poo falling in love with Yum-Yum, a commoner whose father is the national executioner. Tennessee's mother, Edwina Dakin, met his father, Cornelius Williams, while she was appearing in a local Columbus, Mississippi, production of *The Mikado*.

Chapter 2

The Outcasts

To hear Edwina Dakin talk, one would think she was a born and bred Southern belle—flirtatious, charming, and unfailingly proper, with a magnolia-perfect drawl that evoked images of breeding and gentility. Those who met the lively twenty-one-year-old in Columbus, Mississippi, would have been surprised to learn she had been born in the decidedly ungenteel town of Marysville, Ohio.

Edwina's father, the Reverend Walter Dakin, was an Episcopal minister who had uprooted his wife, Rosina, and their daughter at least a half dozen times while she was growing up, in search of ever more comfortable surroundings and amenities. His transient lifestyle was difficult on his only child, so he tried to make up for it by doting on her and indulging her whims, such as allowing her to perform in amateur plays and showering her with trinkets and surprise gifts.

The family eventually settled in Columbus, where Edwina enjoyed the notoriety and attention of being the pretty—and available—daughter of the local minister. She was socially active and attended many dances, where she would bask in the attention of her many gentlemen callers.

While performing in a local production of *The Mikado*, she was introduced by mutual friends to Cornelius Coffin Williams. Although called C.C. by all his friends, Edwina insisted on calling him the more proper sounding Cornelius. Williams was in Columbus on business for the Cumberland Telephone Company.

Cornelius's mother, Isabel, had died of tuberculosis when she was thirty-one, leaving the young boy and his two sisters in the care of their father. He sent Cornelius and his younger sister, Belle, to live in a seminary. When he was older, Cornelius dropped out of the University of Tennessee, where he was majoring in law, to join the military. He earned the rank of second lieutenant while serving in the Spanish-American War. When he finished his enlistment, Cornelius found work at the phone company, which led to his fateful trip to Columbus, Ohio, where he attended a performance of *The Mikado* and became smitten with the vivacious Edwina Dakin.

For the next year and a half, Cornelius courted Edwina, traveling to and from Memphis as his schedule permitted. Finally, he proposed and Edwina accepted. Considering that most of her friends and contemporaries were already married and starting families, Edwina—and her parents—must have been relieved that her bachelorette days were finally over. The couple were married June 2, 1907, in her father's church. They left Columbus to live in Gulfport, where Cornelius was based as a manager for the phone company.

When she was pregnant with their first child, Edwina returned to Columbus to stay with her parents after Cornelius lost his job. He visited regularly, but after their daughter, Rose, was born, they continued to live separate lives and Edwina resumed her social life in Columbus. They seemed to be married in name only.

However, they saw each other enough that Edwina was soon pregnant again. Cornelius eventually took a job as a traveling salesman peddling men's clothing and shoes, which would keep him on the road a majority of the time. Edwina and Rose moved in with her parents full-time.

Cornelius would visit his family every couple of weeks, but the visits became more and more unpleasant. He began staying out late and would show up at the rectory drunk and combative. There were suggestions that he was gambling and seeing other women on the side. This was during a time when polite people didn't discuss "family troubles," so the Reverend Dakin and his wife looked the other way. Edwina was left to deal with her husband on her own.

As time went on, her anger over his behavior turned to fear. When their first son, Thomas Lanier Williams III, was born on March 26, 1911, he entered the world into a family brittle with tension and parents emotionally distanced from one another.

Although Rose was initially resentful of her baby brother, and their temperaments were quite different, before long they became inseparable. Tom was easygoing and quiet, while Rose had a quick temper. Still, they shared an innate understanding and acceptance of one another, even at a young age. Their closeness also stemmed in part from their nomadic lifestyle. When Tom was a toddler, Reverend Dakin accepted a new pastorate in Nashville and moved his wife, daughter, and grandkids to Tennessee. Two years later, they stayed briefly at a church in Canton, Mississippi, before settling in Clarksdale.

Clarksdale has the distinction of being considered the home of the Mississippi blues; it is a quintessential Southern town. Feeling completely in her element, Edwina flourished and immersed herself into the local social scene while Tom and Rose entertained one another.

When he was five, Tom contracted diphtheria, which is a serious bacterial infection usually spread from person to person, much like the flu is transmitted. Today, the disease is extremely rare because children are vaccinated for it, but the vaccine wasn't introduced until 1921. In the early part of the twentieth century, it was a dangerous, sometimes fatal, illness. Symptoms include sore throat, fever, and weakness. Severe cases could lead to paralysis and heart failure.

In her autobiography, *Remember Me to Tom,* Edwina recalled tending to her seriously ill son. "I slept with him for nine nights, following the doctor's direction to keep his throat packed in ice, changing the ice all night, so he would not choke to death."[1]

When his fever finally went down, Edwina allowed Tom out of bed but realized he was unable to walk. The doctor diagnosed him with Bright's disease, now called nephritis, which is an inflammation of the kidneys. He said the boy's leg muscles had become weakened to the point of near paralysis. For nearly two years, Tom could not walk and had to stay indoors.

Prior to his illness, he had been extremely active and loved running around their neighborhood with the other kids. Now, unable to leave the house, he turned inward, losing himself in books and making up stories for fun. Edwina spent all her free time with Tom, a hovering mother hen. Lucy Freeman, who cowrote Edwina's memoirs, noted, "She would never let him forget she saved his life. It was probably the first great dramatic performance he saw, her rendition of his childhood illnesses and her nursing duties."[2]

When she wasn't reminding Tom of all she did for him, Edwina would often tell him stories of her youth. Williams biographer Lyle Leverich wrote, "Over and over again, she would tell Tom about garden parties and cotillions and her gentlemen callers, until he could recite the stories by rote. She said that in those days she saw only 'the charming, gallant, cheerful side' of her smiling bridegroom who had been a telephone man 'in love with long distance.'"[3]

By the time his legs had regained their strength, he was a changed person, more introverted than before. Edwina had also changed, becoming overprotective of her son.

Throughout Tom's ordeal and after, Cornelius was seldom around. Reverend Dakin became a surrogate father to both children, particularly Tom. Edwina later recalled how her son "adored his grandfather. He was always running along at Father's heels when he paid calls on sick parishioners, part of his duties. I would watch out the window as they walked away from the rectory, my father who, although not tall, gave the impression of height because he carried himself so erectly, and the little boy trying to keep up with him, proud that his grandfather would allow him to be company."[4]

Tom's closest companion remained Rose. He would later recall their time in Clarksdale with dreamy nostalgia:

> Before I was eight my life was completely unshadowed by fear. . . . My sister and I were gloriously happy. We sailed paper boats in wash-tubs of water, cut lovely colored paper-dolls out of huge mail-order catalogs, kept two white rabbits under the back porch, baked mud pies in the sun upon the front walk, climbed up and slid down the big wood pile, collected from neighboring alleys and trash-piles bits of colored glass that were diamonds and rubies and sapphires and emeralds.[5]

But their charmed life in Clarksdale with their grandparents would come to an abrupt and jolting end. In the summer of 1918, Edwina announced that she was pregnant—and that Cornelius had accepted an office job as sales manager at the International Shoe Company's St. Louis branch. They would be leaving immediately. Cornelius told his wife that he wanted to give her and the kids a more stable home life and wanted to be more involved with the new baby than he had been with Rose and Tom.

Although his children had seen little of Cornelius, Tom had formed a definite sense about the man, especially when compared to his grandfather:

> My grandfather was a kind man. He was soft spoken and gentle. Somehow he created about the whole house an atmosphere of sweetness and light. Every one in the house seemed to be under his spell. It was a spell of perfect peace. There were no angry scenes, no hard words spoken.
>
> Only on those occasional week-ends when my father visited the house were things different. Then the spell of perfect peace was broken. A loud voice was heard, and heavy footsteps. Doors were slammed. Furniture was kicked and banged. . . . Often the voice of my father was jovial or boisterous. But sometimes it was harsh. And sometimes it sounded like thunder.
>
> He was a big man. Beside the slight, gentle figure of my grandfather, he looked awfully big. And it was not a benign bigness. You wanted to shrink away from it, to hide yourself.[6]

Nobody seemed happy about leaving Clarksdale. Although she had doubts that Cornelius had what it took to be an involved father, Edwina had little choice. It's ironic that in his effort to make a home for his children, Cornelius was ripping them away from the only home they had ever known. Williams would later observe that his father had also removed himself "from the freedom and wildness on which his happiness depended."[7]

He would ultimately take out his resulting unhappiness on his captive family.

The Mikado

The Mikado is one of the most popular operettas ever written. Unlike operas, which tend to be highly dramatic and in which all the dialogue is usually sung, operettas are primarily light operas with the performers speaking occasional lines. Operettas were the precursors of the modern musical comedy, which are plays with songs incorporated to advance the plot.

First presented on March 14, 1885, at London's Savoy Theatre, *The Mikado* is set in the fictional town of Titipu and tells the story of a Japanese prince, Nanki-Poo. The prince falls in love with Yum-Yum, the daughter of the national executioner, and wants to marry her. The show would run for 672 performances. It remains one of the most performed plays by amateur theater companies and school drama departments.

The Mikado is by far the most popular operetta written by the team of dramatist William Gilbert and composer Arthur Sullivan. Although both were successful prior to their collaborations, together Gilbert and Sullivan would become world famous.

Gilbert was born in London in 1836 and had his first taste of drama at a young age. His father was a naval surgeon who was stationed in Italy.

When William was two years old, he was kidnapped by a band of bandits. His family paid the demanded ransom and the toddler was safely returned.

By comparison, the rest of his childhood was uneventful. After finishing school he enlisted in the military. Instead of following in his father's footsteps, he left the service and took a government job pushing paper and found himself bored to distraction. When an aunt died and left him money, Gilbert quit his job and went back to school to study law. However, once he set up practice, he

William Gilbert

22

realized he didn't want to spend his life in court. His career as an attorney was also short-lived.

Several years earlier, Gilbert had begun writing articles and verses for a popular magazine called *Fun*. Instead of signing his real name, he used the pseudonym Bab. Deciding this was his true calling, he turned to writing full-time after quitting law. His first produced play, *Uncle Baby*, opened at the Royal Lyceum Theatre in October 1863. Two more plays followed in 1866, and in 1869 he began an association with a small theater. In addition to writing half a dozen plays that the theater put on, Gilbert also was allowed to start directing. He became known for pushing the boundaries of what was considered acceptable subject matter and dialogue. He is credited with opening doors that in later years would benefit controversial playwrights such as Oscar Wilde and George Bernard Shaw.

In 1871, Gilbert was introduced to a well-known British composer named Arthur Sullivan. A child prodigy, Sullivan mastered several musical instruments by the time he was ten. At eight, he had composed his first song. Starting at fourteen, he won numerous scholarships to some of Europe's most prestigious academies. When he was just nineteen he wrote *The Tempest*, which premiered in April 1862. He quickly became regarded as the leading British composer of his time.

Arthur Sullivan

He first dabbled in comic opera five years later, collaborating with dramatist FC Brunand, and enjoyed the challenge of marrying words to music. When the owner of the Gaiety Theatre commissioned him and William Gilbert to compose a comic opera for his theater, Sullivan readily accepted. The result was *Thespis*, in which the gods on Mount Olympus, now old men and women, take a vacation on Earth and leave a troupe of actors to take their place until they return.

Although *Thespis* came and went without much notice, four years later Gilbert and Sullivan teamed up again for Richard D'Oyly Carte, who managed the Royalty Theatre and needed a one-act operetta to accompany the main opera. *Trial by Jury* was a success and eventually led to a Gilbert, Sullivan and Carte partnership. They formed the Comedy Opera Company to produce all future Gilbert and Sullivan operettas, as well those written by other British collaborators.

The first opera presented under this arrangement was *The Sorcerer* in 1877, followed six months later with *HMS Pinafore*, which would go on to play for two years.

Gilbert and Sullivan mania had arrived. So popular were their operettas that some unscrupulous New York producers were mounting productions without bothering to pay royalties. To correct that oversight, Gilbert and Sullivan sailed to America in 1879. There they premiered *Pirates of Penzance* at the Fifth Avenue Theatre, which became that season's must-see show. Gilbert and Sullivan would become a mainstay on Broadway for years to come.

With money now flooding in, Carte set out to build his own theater, the Savoy. With a seating capacity of 1,300 people, the Savoy was the first theater to use only electric lights. It opened October 10, 1881, with a production of *Patience*, the first of what would become known as the Savoy Operas.

Each new Gilbert and Sullivan opera seemed to be more successful than the last, with *The Mikado* considered by many to be the zenith of their collaborations. However, while the two men made magic in the theater, off stage there was tension and friction. Each found the other arrogant, and the two were intensely competitive, becoming jealous if it was perceived the other was getting more credit for their success. For his contribution to British music, for example, Arthur Sullivan was knighted by Queen Victoria on May 22, 1883.

The flash point occurred over an argument about carpeting. Gilbert, Sullivan, and Carte equally split the expenses for running the Savoy. When Carte installed new carpet for the then costly amount of $500, the frugal Gilbert complained bitterly. When Sullivan sided with Carte, all the pent-up resentment erupted and an ugly, angry exchange followed.

Soon after, Gilbert sent Sullivan the now-famous note dissolving their partnership:

> The time for putting an end to our collaboration has at last arrived. In accordance, therefore, with the contents of my note to you of this morning, I am writing a letter to Carte (of which I enclose a copy) giving him notice that he is not to produce or perform any of my libretti after Christmas 1890. In point of fact, after the withdrawal of *The Gondoliers*, our united work will be heard in public no more.[8]

The announcement was more stunning at the time than the breakup of the Beatles would be in the next century. In 1893, the rift was briefly mended and they collaborated on *Utopia Limited*, but it was clear to both men that the magic was gone. After *The Grand Duke* in 1896, they parted ways permanently, and one of the most successful theater partnerships was over.

Sullivan's world seemed to collapse as well. He had suffered from kidney stones much of his life and was in almost constant, agonizing pain that not even morphine could ease. He began gambling and fell further into ill health after contracting bronchitis. He died home alone in London from heart failure on November 22, 1900. Richard D'Oyly Carte passed away four months later.

Gilbert was eventually knighted by King Edward in 1907. He died four years later at the age of seventy-four, trying to save a drowning woman.

After arriving in St. Louis, the Williamses moved into an apartment on Westminster Place. Although located on a nice street and big enough for the children to have their own rooms, the apartment was dark and depressing.

Chapter 3

A Difficult Transition

Edwina and her children arrived in St. Louis in the summer. Although they were used to humid summers after living in the South, being in a city was shockingly stifling. The buildings blocked the breeze and the concrete streets and sidewalks acted as reflectors, magnifying the intensity of the heat.

At the time, St. Louis was America's fourth largest city and prided itself on being the shoe manufacturing capital of the world. The family was initially forced to stay at a boardinghouse because Edwina came down with the mumps, having contracted the neck- and throat-swelling disease from Tom. Between her pregnancy and the sweltering temperatures, Edwina was forced to bed and was unable to look for housing until she had recovered.

They eventually settled into a furnished apartment on Westminster Place that Tom considered their first family home in St. Louis. Edwina later admitted, "It was a gloomy place . . . it was so dark we had to leave the lights on most of the day, but it was no tenement. Rose's bedroom boasted white furniture, and I added pink curtains. No doubt, to an eight-year-old boy suddenly cut off from the spaciousness of a house and garden, the apartment loomed grim. It was long and narrow, six rooms and a bath, and Tom said he was allotted the worst room, a tiny bedroom off a side hall, but at least he had a room of his own."[1]

Initially at least, Tom and Rose seemed to blend in with the neighborhood kids. He described their block as "a pleasant residential street lined with great trees which made it almost Southern in appearance. Rose and I made friends and we had an agreeable children's life among them, playing hide-and-seek and fly, sheep, fly and bathing under garden hoses in the hot summer. We were only a block from the Lorelei swimming pool and the West End Lyric movie and we had bicycle races about the block."[2] They would also play with Rose's prized collection of small glass animals.

In the dead of winter, on February 21, 1919, Walter Dakin Williams was born, named for Edwina's father, although nobody ever called him Walter. Where Cornelius was inattentive and aloof from Rose and Tom, from the beginning he seemed to dote on Dakin—favoritism not lost on his elder son.

Shortly after giving birth, Edwina contracted the Spanish flu. Also called *La Grippe,* this strain was extremely deadly and turned into a global pandemic. Between 1918 and 1919, it is estimated that over 25 million people died, making it one of the deadliest pandemics in the history of mankind. It was an avian flu similar to the modern bird flu. It was so lethal that more American soldiers died in World War I from the Spanish flu than from battle wounds.

Cornelius was worried enough about his wife's health that he took her with him on a business trip out West for two weeks so she could recuperate in a warmer climate. However, not even their time away alone could mend their mutual resentments. According to biographer Donald Spoto, when their parents returned home from their trip, it was clear Edwina still hadn't recovered, and "there was something else that struck Tom and Rose about their parents. The cool politeness that characterized Cornelius's visits to his family in the South, the enigmatic distance that seemed to separate him emotionally from his wife and children, and Edwina's resentment of his drinking and gambling and carousing—these now seemed to have frozen the couple in a mutual hostility."[3]

That never-ending, underlying chill made the dank Westminster Place apartment even more oppressive—and their mutual alienation from their father further strengthened their bond. Not surprisingly, Dakin grew up feeling left out. He later revealed, "I never really had a close relationship with [my brother] because I was eight years younger, and [he] and Rose were only two years apart. Of course, they wouldn't want their little brother tagging along everywhere they went."[4]

Tom also sought out his sister's unconditional acceptance in the face of ongoing bullying at school. Classmates at the Eugene Field Elementary School made fun of his thick Southern accent, and he was further taunted because of his inability to participate in sports. Although there was never any medical evidence that Tom had suffered heart damage as a result of his bout with diphtheria, Edwina was convinced that strenuous activity would put her son at risk.

Had Tom cared more, he might have fought his mother on the point, but he seemed content to bury himself in books—a pastime that embittered his father. Perhaps sensing his son was "different," Cornelius responded to his lack of athleticism with sneering contempt, and started calling him "Miss Nancy," the implication clear.

For reasons unclear to Tom, the family left Westminster Place and rented a less gloomy apartment on South Taylor. Even though the surroundings were brighter, the move proved socially disastrous for both Tom and Rose. It also marked the first time Tom felt poor, imbuing him with a sense of alienation, of being an outsider.

"It was a radical step down the social scale, a thing we'd never had to consider in Mississippi, and all our former friends dropped us completely—St. Louis being the kind of place where location of residence was of prime importance . . . the malign exercise of snobbery in 'middle American' life was an utterly new experience to Rose and to me and I think its sudden and harsh discovery had a very traumatic effect on our lives. It had never occurred to us that material disadvantages could cut us off from friends. It was about this time, age eleven or twelve, that I started writing stories."[5]

It was also around this time that Tom met Hazel Kramer. Although two years younger, Tom felt an immediate kinship with Hazel, and they soon began spending all their time together. They shared a passion for making up stories and would sit in her attic letting their imaginations loose. Tom was aware his mother did not approve of the friendship, but Hazel remained his best friend through high school. While Tom would later describe their relationship as romantic, it was never sexual, for reasons that would eventually become clear.

Hoping to encourage her son's writing ambitions, Edwina saved up and bought him a secondhand typewriter for ten dollars. Writing became the one positive constant in Tom's life—making bearable the less heartening constant moving and endless arguments about money between his parents.

Edwina estimated they moved nine times over the course of several years. "In one apartment Tom said we slept on everything but the kitchen table, which was practically true. Rose slept on a folding bed in the living room and Tom on one in the dining room. Although I tried to get out of there as quickly as possible because such close quarters makes it difficult for people to get along, we had to remain almost two years."[6]

Life with Cornelius remained strained and uncertain. Nobody ever knew when he would come home drunk and fly into a rage over the slightest annoyance. The only person he seemed to enjoy was Dakin, and the two would often sit together listening to baseball games on the radio. By the time Tom started high school, his relationship with his father was practically nonexistent, and the constant battles between his parents only seemed to fuel his writing. Rose, however, didn't have such an outlet.

As their parents' relationship disintegrated, Tom and Rose increasingly turned to each other for companionship and support. Their younger brother, Dakin, says he always felt like the odd man out because of how close his siblings were. Tom's love for Rose, and his guilt over her emotional problems, would later become the inspiration for *The Glass Menagerie*.

After Edwina suffered a miscarriage in 1921, her health became fragile. Throughout Tom's teen years, she was in and out of hospitals. Rose's worry for her mother bordered on the frantic. Her greatest fear was that Edwina would die, leaving her to deal with her father alone.

Tom avoided Cornelius as much as possible, and writing became a passion. He sat at his typewriter every day, often late into the night, composing poems and stories he would send to magazines in hopes of being published. A month after his sixteenth birthday, Tom's essay "Can a Good Wife Be a Good Sport?" won third place in a contest held by *Smart Set* magazine. His prize was five dollars, but the value of the affirmation was priceless.

That same year, he earned thirty-five dollars when *Weird Tales* bought his short story "The Vengeance of Nitocris," about an Egyptian queen who avenges the murder of her brother. The story was published in August 1928, the same month Reverend Dakin took Tom to Europe on vacation as part of a group excursion with his parish.

While Tom was enjoying his first taste of success, Rose's life seemed a never-ending struggle to keep herself on steady ground. Things seemed to be looking up when she was allowed to attend junior college in Vicksburg, Mississippi. She was bitterly disappointed when Cornelius pulled her out of school and sent her to his family's hometown of Knoxville, Kentucky, for her debut. A debut is when a young woman is "presented" to society, presumably in order to meet eligible young men. Rose's debut was a disaster.

"She was from out of town so no one came," Dakin later remembered. Then while at the station waiting for her train home, "Apparently she was approached by a drifter, who made a pass at her or said something vulgar, and by the time she got back to St. Louis she was almost hysterical."[7]

Edwina was at a loss as to how to help her daughter. Although Rose had dated occasionally, there was nobody serious in her life. She seldom went out socially with friends and spent more and more time staring out the window. She also began worrying about being poisoned and became argumentative with Cornelius. But she also feared him, having witnessed a terrible confrontation between her parents after Tom had left for college. Edwina later described the frightening scene:

One night, after he obviously had been drinking, he walked into the bathroom where I was standing and threatened angrily, "I'm going to kill you!"

I fled in terror into my bedroom and quickly locked the door. He pounded on it as he kept shouting, "Come out of there. I'm going to kill you!" He was almost six feet tall and very stocky, almost fat from all the drinking, and he broke down the door. It struck me and I fainted, mostly from fear.[8]

On another occasion, Rose had wanted to invite a young man to the house. Cornelius spoiled her plans by refusing to give her any privacy in the living room, so Rose canceled the date. Before going to her room, she angrily confronted her father. Irate at her impudence, he slapped her. "She burst into tears and ran out into the street,"[9] Edwina reported.

Then hope arrived in the guise of a handsome, ambitious young man who worked at her father's shoe company as a junior executive. At the time, Cornelius was still highly regarded and on track to rise through the managerial ranks, so her suitor had heard nothing but good things about Rose's father.

They began dating and were soon seeing each other several times a week. Rose would wait by the phone for his call and her whole demeanor would brighten when she heard his voice. It seemed Rose was finally "going steady" and it must be assumed she—and Edwina—had marriage on their minds. Then her father became implicated in a local scandal that would have devastating consequences.

"There had been a sex party . . . among some of the employees of International Shoe," Dakin Williams recalled. "My father and another employee . . . contracted gonorrhea from a prostitute. . . . It was only because Dad told the truth that he was allowed to keep his job once the word got out at the office."[10]

Today, most women would pack their bags, gather up their children, and leave—or at the very least demand her husband seek counseling. Edwina did neither, later claiming divorce was against her religion. Maybe so, but separation and intervention weren't. Her failure to take any action that would force Cornelius to take consequences for his behavior guaranteed the problem would only worsen.

In *Tom: The Unknown Tennessee Williams*, author Lyle Leverich describes an incident in which Cornelius got into a fight with a salesman at his company. Not only did he lose any chance of being promoted, he also lost part of his ear when the salesman bit it off.

"Cornelius was not just a hard drinker, as he liked to think of himself, but in truth, clinically alcoholic," Leverich writes. "He was resorting to what were open secrets within the family: the familiar, but what he thought to be clever, deceptions, such as hiding a bottle behind the bathtub or in other dark corners. He was on an irreversible course towards self-destruction. No one knew why. Edwina . . . contended that it was because he was a bridled aristocrat. His sisters felt it was because of their mother's early death. Dakin said it was because he liked gin."[11]

Whatever the reason, the result was clear. The young man stopped calling and Rose felt her heart turn to cracked glass. Soon after, she began exhibiting physical symptoms such as chronic stomach pains.

Tom was graduated from high school in January 1929. He originally planned to attend University of the South, but those plans fell through. As it turned out, he was lucky to go to college at all. Whether because he disliked his son or had squandered all his money on booze and gambling, at the last minute Tom was informed there was no money for tuition. However, his grandparents came to the rescue and paid the $1,000 to enroll him at the University of Missouri (UM) at Columbia.

According to Edwina, Hazel had wanted to attend UM, but Cornelius decided she would be a distraction for Tom. Cornelius warned Hazel's grandfather, who worked under him, that his job might be in jeopardy if he didn't fix the situation. In the end, Hazel wound up at the University of Wisconsin. Even though they got together during school breaks, Hazel and Tom began to drift apart and eventually lost touch.

There's no small irony in Cornelius's concern that his son would be distracted by Hazel . . . or by any girl. College would afford Tom the freedom and opportunity to finally discover his true sexual identity. It was a revelation that would profoundly impact and inform everything he wrote.

Early Twentieth-Century Literary Magazines

By the time Tennessee Williams entered the contest sponsored by *Smart Set*, the magazine had long been considered one of the leading literary publications in America. Originally founded in 1900 as a general-interest monthly, *Smart Set* enjoyed it's most successful days from 1914 to 1923 under the guidance of editors H.L. Mencken and George Jean Nathan, two of the best-known writers in the country.

Smart Set Magazine

Henry Louis Mencken was born in 1880 in Baltimore, Maryland, where his grandfather and father ran a successful cigar factory. Bowing to family expectations, Mencken went to work at the factory after graduating from high school. When his father died, H.L. chose to pursue a newspaper career and got his first job at the Baltimore *Morning Herald*. He worked his way up to editor at the *Evening Herald*.

In 1906, he joined the staff of the *Baltimore Sun*. A prolific writer, when he wasn't writing for the paper, he composed poems and authored books. As he got older, Mencken's columns became increasingly political. Looking for an outlet with more creative freedom than offered by newspapers, he agreed to sign on as editor of *The Smart Set* along with well-known theater critic George Jean Nathan.

Nathan, who was born in Fort Wayne, Indiana, enjoyed a worldly childhood. His father's family was French, so every other summer, Nathan and his family would vacation in Europe. He attended Cornell University, and his first job out of college was with the *New York Herald* as a junior features reporter. Two years later, he submitted a play review and was named one of the paper's critics.

He soon tired of newspaper work and began freelancing for magazines. He joined *Smart Set* in 1908 as its full-time drama critic and struck up a friendship with the magazine's book reviewer, H.L. Mencken. When Mencken became the publication's editor, Nathan shared the title. Together they set out to create a haven for intellectuals and literary artists.

The Smart Set attracted both unknown and established writers—such as Eugene O'Neill, Jack London, and D.H. Lawrence—because of the editors' willingness to publish controversial and offbeat plays and fiction. The magazine—which had the slogan "One civilized reader is worth a thousand boneheads" in its masthead—reached a small but highly influential audience and helped set literary trends until Mencken and Nathan stepped down as editors in 1923.

A year later, Nathan and Mencken founded American Mercury, which followed in the Smart Set literary tradition. Many of the most important writers of the twentieth century—James M. Cain, William Faulkner, F. Scott Fitzgerald, Sherwood Anderson, and Sinclair Lewis—were all featured in the magazine. When the Great Depression hit, both American Mercury and Smart Set went into decline. Smart Set ceased publishing in 1930. Mencken resigned from American Mercury in 1933, but the magazine survived through numerous owners—and many changes in content—until its final issue in 1980.

George Jean Nathan would go on to become one of the most influential—and hated—New York theater critics. He liked very few productions and his reviews were often scathing. Although years later Tennessee Williams would refer to the critic as his nemesis, Nathan's reaction to The Glass Menagerie was neither enthusiastic nor derisive . . . perhaps because Nathan's girlfriend at the time was Julie Haydon, the actress starring as Laura in the play.

Although Smart Set might have been the most influential literary magazine of its day and the most daring, there were other important magazines featuring writers during the 1930s. The Saturday Evening Post, which by 1937 was selling over three millions issues a week, regularly featured popular fiction. The magazine, however, is probably still best known for commissioning a cover from a young, unknown artist in 1916 named Norman Rockwell, who would go on to be one of America's best-known artists. In all, he created 321 original covers for the Saturday Evening Post.

The New Yorker started out as a sophisticated humor magazine but quickly earned a reputation for its investigative reporting and fiction. Founded by Harold Ross in 1925, the magazine is also credited with popularizing—and legitimizing—short stories as a literary art form. To this day, it publishes one short story every issue.

First Row—WILLIAMS, FERRING, TRYSON, KEALHOFER, SCHWEIG, GUIDRY.
Second Row—CLARK, LORENZ, DUSARD, EXTEIN, PICKERING, HOTCHNER.

After recuperating from a severe bout of exhaustion, Williams returned to college, attending Washington University in St. Louis. While there he formed the St. Louis Poets Workshop with some fellow students and also joined the staff of the campus' *Eliot Review* literary magazine, which posed for the 1936-37 year book. (Williams is circled, second from left.)

Chapter 4

Season in Hell

The University of Missouri, located 150 miles from St. Louis in Columbus, offered Williams the chance to finally be out from under the shadow of his father—whom he referred to as "Big Daddy." He found lodging in a men-only boardinghouse near campus. Next door was the women's building. Although men and women dined together, any other contact between the sexes was forbidden.

A month into the first term, Williams pledged with the fraternity Alpha Tau Omega, mostly to please his father. He moved out of the boardinghouse into the fraternity house, with his grandmother again helping pay his housing costs. Cornelius sent his son the bare minimum of an allowance, and Tom didn't have enough money to buy clothes. He would frequently sneak into another frat brother's room, take a shirt to wear to dinner (where formal dress was required), then sneak it back. He would also write checks from an empty account to pay for restaurant bills.

For as frustrating as his financial situation was, his writing was earning him attention. The university newspaper wrote a feature about him in October 1929, with the headline "Shy Freshman Writes Romantic Love Tales for Many Magazines." The article divulged the following:

> At 17 years of age, Tom Williams of St. Louis . . . received $35 from the *Smart Set* magazine for an article on "The Type of Woman a Man

Wants to Marry." Mr. Williams . . . has had a number of stories published in *Weird Tales* and *Smart Set* magazines.

He likes to write love stories best and declares that he does not get his inspiration from actual experience but rather from reading a wide variety of authors. Louis Bromfield is his favorite author. . . .

It bothers Mr. Williams to have anyone ask him questions about himself. He is little more than five feet tall. He has clean cut features and smooth brown hair. His eyes, which have a look that seems thousands of miles away, add to the unapproachable and reserved appearance which he presents. He is equally as reticent and shy as he appears and feels that his having stories published is nothing out of the ordinary. . . .

He intends to enter the School of Journalism. . . .[1]

Those plans were about to change. After seeing a production of Henrik Ibsen's play *Ghosts*, Williams had an epiphany. He wanted to try his hand at playwriting. It quickly became apparent that Tom had a natural gift for the form.

He entered a writing competition sponsored by the Dramatic Arts Club. His play about the life of a South Pacific missionary, *Beauty Is the Word*, received an honorable mention, making Williams the first freshman ever to be so recognized.

After completing the first year of college, Williams returned home for the summer. America was in the initial grip of the Great Depression, but Tom found work selling magazine subscriptions door to door.

When he returned to college, Williams fell in love—with one of his fraternity brothers. Although the relationship was never consummated, mostly because of Tom's shyness as opposed to lack of desire, it confirmed that Williams's attraction to men was not a passing curiosity but part of who he was. Years later he would observe, "Sexuality is a basic part of my nature. I never considered my homosexuality as anything to be disguised. Neither did I consider it a matter to be over-emphasized. I consider it an accident of nature."[2]

That awareness no doubt contributed to Tom's shyness and duck-out-of-water reputation. Frat brother Elmer Lower remembers Williams as being "too shy to ask a girl for a date so [fellow brother] Harold Mitchell and I had to find someone for him so we could have a triple date for a dance or sports event. Tom wasn't a typical frat man or buddy, and he seemed awkward in groups, even during the simple and brief socializing that was permitted when we brought girls back to the frat house living room for a while."[3]

He added, "None of us ever had an inkling of homosexual tendencies in him or his roommate during those years. . . . Heterosexual sex was rare enough and mysterious enough and alternatives weren't even a topic for conversation."[4]

It would be several more years before Williams would openly pursue his sexuality. Until then, his passion remained writing. He began racking up dozens of absences, missing classes at will to stay home and work on his stories. His grades suffered from his indifference, giving Cornelius an excuse to pull him out of college.

The break point came when Williams failed his Reserve Officer Training Corps (ROTC) class. His father took it as a personal affront and demanded Tom drop out. Both Dakin and Edwina revealed that while Cornelius was furious over Tom's grades, the real reason he made Tom quit college was financial—by 1932, the Great Depression was in full swing and money was tight. Williams returned home and took a summer job at the shoe company, where he ran errands, did paperwork, dusted shoes, and delivered samples.

Although in later life Williams would tell people he worked at the company for three years, he actually worked a total of ten months on staff *over the course of three years*. After his initial summer job, Tom lived at home passing the time mostly reading and writing—and taking evening classes his father insisted on to learn secretarial skills that might help him land a permanent job.

Regardless of what he might have had to do to earn money, in his heart Tom thought of himself as a writer. During his time back in St. Louis, he produced an astonishing amount of poetry and prose. His verse was proving especially successful and was published in numerous magazines across the country, earning him notoriety as a poet.

He went back to the company full-time in late June 1934, after which Williams's life took on a grueling routine. After working all day at the factory, Williams would come home and stay up late into the night writing, often not

39

even bothering to take the time to eat. Then he would drag himself out of bed in the morning and start the routine all over. His discipline never wavered. He wrote one story a week, which he would religiously send off to *Story* magazine.

Edwina recalled Tom once saying, "I wrote not with any hope of making a living at it, but because I found no other means of expressing things that seemed to demand expression. There was never a moment when I did not find life to be immeasurably exciting to witness, however difficult it was to sustain."[5]

Eventually, Tom crashed. In March 1935, two days before his twenty-fourth birthday, he took Rose to see *The Scarlet Pimpernel* at the movies. On the way home he had an attack of tachycardia, or rapid heart beat. When his hands went numb, he thought he was having a heart attack, and he and Rose took a cab to St. Luke's Episcopal Hospital.

Terrified, Rose called home to tell Edwina that Tom had just suffered a stroke. The diagnosis was exhaustion, exacerbated by high blood pressure. The doctor kept Williams in the hospital for a week before discharging him. Tom would recover, but the incident seemed to catapult Rose over the emotional edge. Shortly after returning home, Williams remembers his sister suggesting they all die together. Another time she became hysterical, warning her father he was going to be murdered.

Rose had already been hospitalized briefly and was seeing a psychiatrist, but nothing slowed her mental deterioration. There were periods of remission, during which she would seem more in touch and would even look for work. But those windows of optimism became shorter and less frequent until they would disappear altogether. Between Rose's mental health, Tom's frail health, Cornelius's alcoholism, and Edwina's smothering mothering, the family was on the verge of imploding.

Tom never returned to the shoe company. He tendered his resignation and it was decided he should spend the summer getting his strength back by recuperating at his grandparents' home in Memphis. Free from the oppressive atmosphere of his family home, Tom once again came alive.

He collaborated on a play with Dorothy Shapiro, the daughter of his grandparents' neighbors. *Cairo, Shanghai, Bombay* was a comedy about two sailors on a double date. The play was staged by a local theater company, the

Rose Arbor Players, and was well received. After hearing the audience laughing at his dialogue, Williams knew that his destiny was to be a playwright.

Refreshed and revitalized, Tom returned to St. Louis in September and audited some classes at nearby Washington University. There he became friends with poet Clark Mills, who was extremely supportive of Tom's abilities. "Tom had fanatical and inexhaustible energy in his writing," Mills said later. "His persistence was almost grotesque . . . demoniac. He wasn't aiming basically at material success. He wrote because it was a fatal need."[6]

In 1935, along with another college buddy, William Smith, Mills and Tom formed the St. Louis Poets Workshop, which was essentially the three of them sitting around talking about writing. That year, Williams had seven more poems published. His success, however, did nothing to improve his social skills.

Smith described his friend as "the shyest, quietest person I had ever met. His stony-faced silence often put people off; he appeared disdainful of what was going on around him, never joining in the quick give-and-take of a conversation. He would sit quietly in a gathering for long periods of time until suddenly like a volcano erupting he would burst out with a high cackle and then with resounding and uncontrollable laughter. Those who knew him well found this trait delightful, but to others it seemed rude and disconcerting."[7]

Williams enrolled as a full-time Washington University student in the fall of 1936. His classes included literature, drama, French, and Greek. Around this time Williams discovered the work of poet Hart Crane, who used his own past and life experiences as the basis for his art. It was impossible for Tom not to feel a strong kinship with Crane: He had grown up in a highly dysfunctional family, was devoted to writing—and was gay. Hart's poetry clearly expressed the alienation he felt being gay and the intolerance he encountered because of it. Hart became an alcoholic and committed suicide by jumping off the SS *Orizaba* somewhere off the Florida coast in 1932.

In his late twenties, Williams was also struggling to fully identify his own sexuality. Today, most major, nonreligious colleges in America have gay and lesbian organizations that provide support and resources for gay students; but in the 1930s, it was still considered taboo to openly and frankly discuss sexuality of *any* kind. For someone struggling to come out of the closet, it was typically a lonely, confusing process. Williams used his writing as an outlet for his feelings of alienation. He already sensed he would always live on the fringe of mainstream society. Rather than fight it, he would eventually embrace it and use it as the emotional foundation for his best work.

In March 1937, the Mummers of St. Louis—a somewhat avant-garde theater company run by director William Holland—staged his first full-length play, *Candles to the Sun*, which became a local success. Later that year the Mummers would also produce another Williams play, *Fugitive Kind*. As is so typical of many artists, all his successes failed to thicken his skin against the disappointments that were sure to come. One such setback occurred when Willliams entered a contest that were sponsored by WU's drama department. He submitted *Me, Vashya!*, an antiwar comedy about an arms dealer.

Because of his growing reputation, many students assumed Williams would win—as did he. When he came in fourth place, he was shocked and embarrassed to anger.

"It was a terrible shock and humiliation to me," he said in 1958. "It was a cruel blow. I had always thought I was shy, but I discarded all humility. I stormed into Carson's office. (He was a good professor.) I screamed at him. I surprised myself."[8]

Typically, Tom had so immersed himself in writing *Me, Vashya!* that he neglected his other classes. When it came time for his Greek final, he was completely unprepared. The morning of the exam, he anguished over the inevitable. He wrote: "Monday. Never woke in more misery in all my life. Intolerable. The brilliant earth mocks my fear. Children and birds sing. People speak in casual voices. The poplar leaves shine. Yet I up here in this narrow room endure torture. God help me! Please! I've got to have help or I'll go mad. What is this a punishment for? What? Or is it all blind, blind without meaning!"[9]

Williams knew that if he failed his exam, he would not be allowed to graduate. As his time at WU ticked away, he wrote a poem he titled *Blue Song* on the back of his test booklet, which begins:

I am tired
I am tired of speech and of action

If you should meet me upon a
street do not question me for
I can tell you only my name
and the name of the town I was
born in—[10]

The existence of the poem only came to light in 2004 after a Washington University Professor, Henry Schvey, discovered it while browsing through a New Orleans bookstore's collection of Williams's documents.

"I knew immediately what it was because it had the [university crest] on it," explained Professor Schvey. "It had the name Th. Williams on the front cover."[11]

Williams's bitterness over *Me, Vashya!* was so intense that he would later remove the play from his list of works and completely expunge his time at WU from his memoirs. In ironic karma that Williams would have appreciated, in 2004 Professor Schvey had resurrected *Me, Vashya!* from the university's archives and premiered it during an international symposium showcasing Williams's early career. Two weeks later he found the poem.

Tom's failure to earn his degree might have created more of an uproar except for the fact that the family was already in so much turmoil over Rose. Her hallucinations had intensified, her angry outbursts were more frequent, and she became preoccupied with sex.

Despite his sister's illness—or perhaps because of it—Williams decided to finish his degree at the University of Iowa. The next time he saw Rose, the unthinkable had happened.

Hart Crane

Brilliant and indulgent, daring and self-destructive, poet Hart Crane is considered one of the most influential literary artists of the modernist movement. *Modernism* refers to the attempt to break free from traditional nineteenth-century style, structure, and form to make literature more relevant to a rapidly changing, technology-driven twentieth-century world. Other modernists include e.e. cummings, Virginia Woolf, Ezra Pound, W.B. Yeats, and Gertrude Stein. Where many modernists' works reflected a post–World War I pessimism and disillusionment, Crane sought to express optimism about the American spirit.

Hart Crane

Harold Hart Crane was born a child of privilege in Garrettsville, Ohio, on July 21, 1899. His father, Clarence, had made a fortune by inventing Life Savers candies, but his emotionally fragile mother, Grace, was miserably unhappy in her marriage. When Hart was nine, Grace suffered a nervous breakdown. He was sent to stay with his maternal grandparents, who introduced him to poetry.

Clarence expected his son to pursue a career in the family business, but by the time Hart was thirteen, he already considered himself a poet. After his parents divorced in 1916, Hart dropped out of high school, and the Cranes grudgingly allowed their son to live in New York.

He got a job selling ads for a poetry magazine and spent his free time in book salons, where he could read his favorite authors and discuss literature with an assortment of fascinating people. Nomadic by nature, Crane never stayed in one place—or held a job—very long. Between 1917 and 1924, he shuttled back and forth between Ohio and New York, holding down a series of unfulfilling jobs, from junior reporter to copyeditor to flunky at his father's factory.

In 1919, while working in one of his father's candy stores in Akron, Ohio, Crane had his first affair with a man. The relationship had a profound effect on him. He believed that his art was intrinsically connected to his sexuality. His mother was a staunch Christian Scientist, so to be gay was to be an outcast. That sense of alienation formed the basis for his creative vision and gave him a unique insight—as an outsider looking in on the mainstream.

Over the next several years, Crane's verses were published by several respected literary magazines. His first collection of poems, *White Buildings*, was published in 1926. Included in the volume are a series of erotic poems, *Voyages I–VI*, which were written during his first true love affair.

When he was twenty-five, Crane fell in love with Emil Opffer, a Danish merchant marine. The affair was passionate, intense—but brief. It would be a pattern Crane would follow his entire life. Some speculate that the disappointment of losing his first love may have convinced Crane that it wasn't possible to find one person with whom to share his life. It's also possible that Crane feared that settling down would take the edge off his poetry. Whatever the reason, Crane chose promiscuity, entering into one loveless affair or one-night stand after another.

Hart's next project took years to finish. Inspired by the Brooklyn Bridge in New York, *The Bridge* is a symbolic vision of America's history and spirit. When the sixty-page poem was published in 1930, it brought Crane instant acclaim—which did little to lessen his erratic behavior and dependency on alcohol.

In 1931 he was awarded a Guggenheim Fellowship to write in Mexico for a year to create an epic poem about the conquests of Hernando Cortés. He rented a villa in Mexico City but drank more than he wrote, producing only a few verses, and suffered bouts of debilitating self-loathing. That same year his father died and a close friend killed himself. Distraught, he drank iodine in a botched suicide attempt.

With his fellowship over and the money gone, Crane left Mexico for the U.S. in April 1932. On the morning of April 27, an inebriated Crane hurled himself off the ship into the Gulf of Mexico. The horrified passenger who witnessed the leap immediately alerted the crew, but the poet had already vanished beneath the waves.

Although he only published two volumes of work, Crane left a legacy that still resonates today.

By the time he enrolled in college, writing had become Tennessee's passion. Originally he concentrated on poetry, but after seeing a production of Henrik Ibsen's play *Ghost*, Williams decided to try his hand at playwriting. Although he had some plays produced locally in St. Louis, national recognition would elude him for many years.

Chapter 5

On the Road

Although many of his stories, such as *27 Wagons Full of Cotton,* had contained evocative sexual innuendo and imagery, Williams admitted he was not yet writing from experience. In a 1973 interview, he revealed, "I was a terrible puritan . . . and remained a terrible puritan until my late 20s. I was a virgin with either sex until the age of 26."[1]

Not long after arriving at the University of Iowa, Williams had his first sexual experience with classmate Bette Reitz, which also happened to be his last physical relationship with a woman in his life. The affair lasted for three months until Bette ended it after they returned from Christmas break, having taken up with another beau.

Initially, Williams was depressed—nobody ever likes getting dumped—but he soon recovered. In his *Memoirs,* Williams recalled, "[Bette] began to fade out of my libido. Others of my own gender began to fade in."[2] For the immediate future, though, he remained unattached to anyone, having more pressing—and distressing—matters on his mind.

During the summer of 1937, Rose had been admitted on several occasions to the state mental facility at Farmington. Edwina was warned that Rose had become a potential danger to herself and possibly to others. One of the doctors even told Cornelius, "Rose is liable to go down and get a butcher knife one night and cut your throat."[3] The concern over Rose hurting her father was mildly ironic considering Cornelius's penchant for abuse.

One night not long after Tom had left for Iowa, Edwina arrived home to find Rose even more hysterical than usual. She claimed that her father, raging drunk, had walked into her room and made sexual advances. Naturally, Edwina would not, could not, even consider that such a thing might have occurred. For two days, Rose remained frantic and inconsolable, so Edwina took her back to Farmington, where several psychiatrists examined her.

"After studying Rose, they advised a lobotomy, which, they said, was a new way of helping the mentally ill," Edwina recalled. "This is a very delicate operation on the brain which destroys the chain of memory, in large part, so that one lives without being tortured by fantasies. However, as I found out, it also causes the loss of that part of the psyche that spurs one on to be independent in body and spirit."[4]

The added incentive was that the operation would be free at Farmington, whereas a private hospital would charge thousands of dollars.

"They tried to make me believe this was the only hope for Rose," Edwina later explained, "that otherwise she would spend the rest of her days a raving maniac in a padded cell."[5]

Cornelius and Edwina consented, and at twenty-eight years old, Rose would lose herself permanently. Although the procedure took away her fear, it also took away her ability to communicate. She was effectively autistic, withdrawn from the world and everyone in it.

Nobody wrote Tom to tell him what had happened to his sister. When he came home for the opening of *Fugitive Kind*, he was blindsided by the news. Distraught and angry, he blamed his mother much more than he did his father, since his father had never really pretended to care for Rose or for him.

"She is the one who approved the lobotomy. . . . She gave permission to have it done while I was away. I think she was frightened most by all of Rose's sexual fantasies. But that's all they were—fantasies! . . ."[6]

"My sister could have become quite well by now if they hadn't performed that goddam operation on her; she would have come back to the surface. My mother panicked because she said my sister had begun using four letter words. *Do anything! Don't let her talk like that!*"[7]

For her part, Edwina insisted the decision had been her husband's and later admitted "the lobotomy for Rose was a grave mistake. We all believed at the time that this operation might completely cure Rose, as we relied on the advice of a local psychiatrist. We had no idea of the permanent damage it is now known to do to the personality. . . .

"I think Tom always felt as though he failed Rose, that had he been on hand when the big decision was made, he might have been able to stop the lobotomy. . . . I think his was a grief beyond words."[8]

Actually, his words are pointedly eloquent. "I failed to properly observe the shadow falling on Rose."[9]

Thirty years later, he was still haunted by his sister's fate. "She was the best of us all, do you understand? More beautiful, more intelligent, sweeter and warmer than anyone. Not one of us was fit to stoop and tie her shoes."[10]

Williams also recognized that Rose's tragedy became the emotional foundation for much of his ensuing work. "I don't think I would have been the poet I am without that anguished familial situation. I've yet to meet a writer of consequence who did not have a difficult familial background if you explored it."[11]

Back in Iowa, Tom returned to college with a heavy heart, but he managed to have enough discipline to make it to most of his classes. Even so, he only mustered Ds in his drama classes, which meant he had to attend summer school. To pay for the extra courses, he took a job washing dishes in the university hospital cafeteria. At least the job provided three meals a day.

It was a lonely couple of months. "I took to wandering aimlessly about the streets at night to escape the stifling heat of my room. There were many great trees and the town had an old-fashioned charm. At night it seemed almost Southern. I was lonely and frightened; I didn't know the next step. I was finally fully persuaded that I was [gay] but had no idea what to do about it."[12]

Williams successfully completed his summer courses, and on August 5, 1938—nine years after he entered college as a freshman—earned his bachelor of arts degree with a major in English. He was twenty-seven, with no job prospects and limited finances. His grandparents couldn't afford to support him and Cornelius, completely opposed to his pursuit of a writing career, *wouldn't* support him.

Tom returned to St. Louis to finish *Not About Nightingales*, which was to be produced by the Mummers. However, the theater group had fallen on hard times and was forced to close, another victim of the Depression.

Trying to find some traction to jump start his professional career and get some cash to live on, he traveled to Chicago in hopes of getting a writing job with the Works Progress Administration. The WPA was one of President Franklin Delano Roosevelt's New Deal programs intended to provide employment to the needy. However, there were only a handful of positions available, and Williams was turned down because his family was not destitute. The Chicago office suggested he try New Orleans, which had more openings and wasn't as strict about family income.

He went back to St. Louis because his grandparents were visiting, then took the bus to New Orleans. There were no jobs in that city, either. Williams ultimately didn't care, because he fell madly in love with New Orleans and decided to stay. He found his own employment, taking whatever came along, from working as a waiter in the French Quarter to handing out flyers for jazz clubs to tourists.

It was the city where Thomas Lanier Williams would reinvent himself. At his boardinghouse, he registered using the name Tennessee Williams. Why Tennessee? Over the years, Williams gave a variety of explanations. Even Edwina wasn't sure which one was true. She wrote:

> One time he told Mark Barron, Associated Press drama critic, "I got the name of Tennessee when I was going to the University of Iowa because the fellows in my class could only remember that I was from a Southern state with a long name. And when they couldn't think of Mississippi, they settled on Tennessee. That was all right with me, so when it stuck, I changed to it permanently."
>
> He also gave as reason that "the Williamses had fought the Indians for Tennessee and I had already discovered that the life of a young writer was going to be something similar to the defense of a stockade against a band of savages."[13]

Biographer Donald Spoto suggested another scenario, dating back to the summer of 1935, which he'd spent at his grandparents' home recuperating from exhaustion. "And so it was not basically from his *father's* family he took the name, but from the cherished summer he linked with a turning from emotional collapse to an emergence as a creator of character and dialogue. In the state of Tennessee, with his beloved grandparents, he had become well enough to write his first play produced outside school and that memory was most deeply responsible for the name some, at the time of its adoption, considered whimsical, ludicrous or hopelessly fey [crazy]."[14]

Williams paid three dollars a week for a room probably little bigger than a walk-in closet. It was located in the heart of the French Quarter, or *Vieux Carré* ("old square"), where literally anything happened. Sensual, lively, audacious, creative, fun, decadent, fascinating, dangerous, and utterly unique, New Orleans was the perfect place for Williams to assert himself artistically and sexually.

Rather than be distracted by the vibrant life surrounding him, Williams was inspired by it. He wrote every day of the people and places he encountered on his travels through the city. Later in his career, Williams would muse on the importance of setting and environment:

> Among the many misapprehensions held about writers is the idea that they follow a peaceful profession, an idea that derives from the fact that most writers have a sedentary appearance and that most writing is done in a more or less stationary position, usually seated in a chair at a table. But writing is actually a violent activity. . . . They find it difficult to remain long in one place, for writing books and taking voyages are corresponding gestures.
>
> If the writer is truly a writer . . . his first concern, when he goes traveling, will be to discover that magic place of all places where the work goes better than it has gone before. For one of the mysterious things about writing is the extreme susceptibility it shows to the influence of places. . . . But sooner or later this particular place will be exhausted for him and he must find another. . . .
>
> America is no longer a terribly romantic part of the world, and writers . . . are essentially romantic spirits—or they would not be writing. Now there are only two cities left in America with a romantic

appeal, however vestigial, and they are, of course, New Orleans and San Francisco.[15]

New Orleans provided the backdrop for Williams's sexual coming of age, and his writing took on a new insight and maturity. "My life was a series of little adventures unconsummated before I was 28," he commented many years later. "It was after I went to New Orleans that I selected homosexuality as a way of sexual life. Lucky for me . . . the decision was made for me.

"No living person doesn't contain both sexes, mine could have been either one. Truly, I have two sides to my nature. All my relationships with women are very, very important to me. . . . I understand women, and I can write about them." That being said, he added, "I could not operate freely as a writer having several wives and a family."[16]

Like Hart Crane, Williams also came to believe his creativity was in no small way tied to his sexuality. "There is no doubt in my mind that there is more sensibility—which is equivalent to more talent—among the gays of both sexes than the 'norms.' Why? They must compensate for so much more."[17]

In February 1939, Williams entered yet another play contest, this time sponsored by The Group Theatre in New York. The Group, formed in 1931, had become one of Broadway's most creative theater companies, dedicated to presenting contemporary plays about the modern human condition. It seemed a perfect fit for Williams's work. There was just one problem—to enter the contest, playwrights had to be under twenty-five years old. For Williams, the solution was simple. He lied about his age and listed his birthday as March 26, 1914, which became his birth date of record in the media. It would take over two decades before some enterprising journalist uncovered the deception.

As Tennessee Williams, he submitted his four full-length plays and a collection of one-acts he titled *American Blues* to the contest. Meanwhile, he was once again faced with the daunting question of how to make money. When one of his fellow boarders offered Williams and his friend Jim Parrott a ride to California, he accepted, naively thinking he might be able to find work as a movie screenwriter. Instead, he went to work on a ranch outside Los Angeles, slaughtering and plucking squab for a month until Cornelius arranged a job for him at an L.A. shoe store.

A week before his birthday, a telegram arrived.

THE JUDGES OF THE GROUP THEATRE PLAY CONTEST ARE HAPPY TO MAKE A SPECIAL AWARD OF ONE HUNDRED DOLLARS TO YOU FOR YOUR FIRST THREE SKETCHES IN AMERICAN BLUES.[18]

Originally, there was only supposed to be one prize, but judge Molly Day Thacher was impressed enough with his one-acts that she requested a special $100 award be given for his collection. A letter from Thacher, along with the check, arrived shortly thereafter. She ended by encouraging Williams to come east.

"I hope the winning of this award will be the beginning of a fruitful association with the Group Theatre, that you will keep us in touch with your work and that it will not be too long before you come to New York to get acquainted at first hand with our theatre. Sincere congratulations from Harold Clurman, Irwin Shaw and from me."[19]

Williams quit the shoe store and, with his award money in hand, headed to Mexico with Jim Parrott. From there, they went to Laguna Beach, California, and rented a cabin. For the first time since arriving on the West Coast, Tennessee pulled out his typewriter. His time in Laguna proved both relaxing and productive. He'd write every morning and work at a bowling alley in the evenings.

Back in New York, Thacher, who was married to actor and up-and-coming director Elia Kazan, had decided to take Williams under her wing. Known for championing new talent, Thacher sent his plays to agent Audrey Wood, who ran the Liebling-Wood Agency with her husband, William Liebling. It would turn out to be a match made in theater heaven.

Impressed with what she read, Wood sent Williams a contract. Not wanting to rush into anything, he stalled. She wrote a second time, urging him to sign the contract. She added that *Story* had bought "The Field of Blue Children," which Wood had submitted on his behalf. It was the first time he was published under the name Tennessee Williams.

Tired of L.A. and anxious to pursue his theater career in earnest, he signed the contract. But the road to Broadway would prove much bumpier—and much longer—than he ever anticipated.

A History of Lobotomies

On Wednesday, September 13, 1848, a group of construction workers were blasting through some mountainous terrain near Cavendish, Vermont. The foreman was an affable twenty-six-year-old man named Phineas T. Gage.

One of Gage's duties was to set explosives into boulders so that they could be blown into smaller, removable pieces. Late that afternoon, a spark accidentally set off an explosion that blew a three-and-a-half-foot, thirteen-pound piece of iron through Gage's head. It entered under his left cheekbone and exited through the top of his skull by the brain's frontal lobe.

Miraculously, Gage survived. He was treated by town physician Dr. John Harlow. Even though his injury destroyed a significant portion of his brain, other than his shattered cheek and a post-injury infection, Gage appeared otherwise physically unaffected. There was no motor impairment, no blindness or blurred vision, no problem talking, no loss of memory.

Despite the doctor's report, when he returned to his home in New Hampshire, people noticed that Phineas had changed. The once friendly, outgoing Irishman was now relentlessly rude, had trouble concentrating, blurted out inappropriate obscenities, was restless and impatient, and engaged in reckless behavior.

Dr. Harlow published a paper about Gage in 1868. It was the first time doctors realized that personal behavior was controlled by the brain's frontal lobe. Subsequently, other physicians reported dramatic personality changes in patients who had suffered frontal lobe traumas. Inevitably, some wondered if erratic behavior of mentally disturbed people might be controlled by intentionally damaging their frontal lobe. In 1890, Dr. Gottlieb Burckhardt put that question to the test.

At his psychiatric hospital, Burckhardt conducted an experiment on six patients that would be unthinkable today—he drilled holes into their brains. Two of the human guinea pigs died. The others survived, although whether or not their behavior significantly changed was unclear. Despite the inconclusiveness, Burckhardt's ghoulish procedure was a harbinger of a disturbing medical trend to come—psychosurgery.

In 1935, neurologist Walter Freeman attended a medical conference in London. He was interested in ways of treating schizophrenia, which at the time was considered a form of dementia. He was intrigued by a presentation about two chimps that had had their frontal lobes completely removed. The result was zoned-out chimps that could not be provoked into any kind of aggressive behavior.

Since biologically chimps and humans share 96 percent of the same DNA, the inference was obvious: If chimps could be made calm by removing their frontal lobes, why couldn't people?

54

Walter Freeman

Later that year, Spanish physician Egas Moniz tested that theory and performed the first leukotomy on humans. A leukotomy is when the nerves connecting the frontal lobe to the rest of the brain are destroyed.

The patients, who had been institutionalized in a mental hospital, suffered numerous side effects but did seem calmer—to the point of being lifeless. Even so, the results were significant enough that Moniz would later receive the 1949 Nobel Prize in medicine.

When he read Moniz's findings, Dr. Freeman saw it as a cure-all. Despite having absolutely no qualifications as a surgeon, Freeman and his associate James Watts began performing psychosurgery in 1936, using a rubber mallet to drive a modified ice pick into the patient's skull right above the eye.

Despite serious reservations within the medical community, the Freeman-Watts Standard Lobotomy became an accepted method for dealing with a variety of mental illnesses, including obsessive-compulsive disorder, depression, schizophrenia, and anything else that seemed otherwise untreatable. Even children were given lobotomies. For some families, the economics of mental illness may have been an incentive—the cost of a lobotomy was $250, while long-term care for the mentally ill would cost thousands every year.

Between 1936 and the late 1950s, it is estimated that 50,000 Americans had been lobotomized—with Freeman notching over 3,400. When one of his patients died after her third ice-pick lobotomy in 1956, Freeman finally had his license revoked.

The unacceptable number of deaths and the often-horrific side-effects eventually discredited lobotomies as a treatment for schizophrenia, but not before the lives of thousands of mentally ill patients, including Rose Williams, had been ruined. What is particularly tragic is that by the mid-1950s, drugs had been developed to treat schizophrenia, allowing many patients to control their symptoms and lead productive lives.

Williams's floundering career got a much needed boost after he won a special award in a playwriting contest sponsored by The Group Theatre. One of the judges, Molly Day Thacher, sent his work to literary agent Audrey Wood who was impressed enough to offer Tennessee a contract. She would remain his agent for over thirty years.

Chapter 6

Breakthrough

Williams's first trip to New York was a lesson in humility. He arrived in the city with precious little cash and no prospects. When he met his agent, she realized her first job was to keep a roof over his head and food on his table.

"His primary need was survival," Audrey Wood recalled in her autobiography. "It was an unending struggle to stay alive and fed until we could find a producer who would give his work a production. Tennessee needed every penny of the sustenance we could find him."[1]

His first benefactor was well-known theater actor Hume Cronyn, who was interested in finding plays to direct and produce. At the urging of Wood, he agreed to option some of Williams's one-acts. But New York was expensive, and Tennessee was forced to go back to St. Louis in November 1939. Every time he was forced to retreat home was a personal humiliation, because then he had to confront his father's disapproval and lack of support.

Battling bouts of depression, he worked furiously on his latest play, *Battle of Angels,* unsure he could continue with this tenuous way of living. His outlook improved considerably in late December when Wood called with good news—he had been awarded a $1,000 writing fellowship, which is a kind of scholarship, by the Dramatists Guild. Wisely, Wood kept control of the purse strings. Rather than send the check to Tennessee, she arranged to give him a monthly allowance.

The money allowed Williams to go back to New York in January 1940. He rented a room at the YMCA on Sixty-third Street by Central Park West. While his agent tried to find a producer for *Battle of Angels*, Tennessee attended a seminar at the New School for Social Research. Ironically, his University of Iowa professor E. C. Mabie was teaching there.

In a letter to his grandfather, Williams sounded content . . . maybe a little *too* content for his own liking. He wrote, "Life here is very pleasant. I get up and take a shower and a quick swim, write several hours, then take another short work-out in the gym, go out for dinner and then attend a play or exchange visits with various interesting people that I have met here. Certainly no stagnation as there is in the middle-west. However I don't think I would stay here while working on another play—there are too many pleasant, enticing distractions. The attic in St. Louis or a cabin on the beach or the desert is best for that purpose."[2]

To his mother, he expressed cautious optimism: "So many interesting things to do that the days slip by unnoticed. I spend every afternoon watching the Group Theatre rehearse. Evenings I usually visit some of the many fascinating people I've met or else take in a new play . . . tonight I went to a poetry reading by W. H. Auden, the most famous English poet, and spent a couple of hours talking to a group of the best New York poets who were also in the audience. . . . I have worked a good deal, however, on the last act of my new play and I have a feeling the Group will be pleased with it. . . . After seeing some of this season's productions I don't see why my work should be neglected much longer by the commercial theatre."[3]

In February, the New School staged a weekend production of Williams's one-act, *The Long Goodbye*. The play's protagonist, Joe, is a struggling writer who reminisces about events from his family's past, which are played out as flashbacks—his mother's agony from cancer and her ultimate suicide, confrontations with a negligent father, and witnessing his sister go from party girl to prostitute. While the circumstances are fictional, it is clear the emotional foundation of the play was born from Williams's own turbulent family life. His sense of loss is also vividly presented when the writer character says: "You're saying goodbye all the time, every minute you live. Because that's what life is, just a long, long goodbye—to one thing after another."[4]

The Long Goodbye is clearly the first of Williams's "memory plays," which he described as having a three-part structure: 1) a character experiences something profound; 2) that experience causes an "arrest of time," and 3) the character must relive that profound experience until sense is made of it. *The Long Goodbye* also previews what would become an overriding theme in Williams's most fully realized work—that strict social mores tend to crush creativity and individuality.

In May of that year, the Theatre Guild optioned *Battle of Angels*. One of the guild's advisers, Paul Bigelow, was a strong supporter of Williams and would become a close, lifelong friend, often letting Tennessee sleep on the couch when he was between rooms.

"He was rootless in New York and never happy there . . . it was never his city," Bigelow told biographer Donald Spoto. "At this time in his life, he had what I can only call an unformed emotional persona and did not deal very well with the pressures of city life."[5]

Also exacerbating his edginess was his failing eyesight. Williams's left eye was developing a cataract, which is a clouding of the eye lens. Although repairable through surgery, it would be years before he could afford medical treatment. Having only one good eye made writing that much more difficult and tiring.

Hoping to regroup, Williams spent the summer and early autumn of 1940 traveling to Provincetown, Rhode Island; Mexico City; and finally back to St. Louis, where he learned *Battle of Angels* had been cast and the guild was ready to proceed with production. Back in New York, he returned to the YMCA and got a job at a Times Square bookstore, having spent all his advance money traveling.

The director chosen by the guild, Margaret Webster, would later admit she didn't think the play was very good as a whole but thought there were flashes of dialogue and subtext present that portended his genius. Certainly, the themes present in *Battle of Angels* would become synonymous with Williams's work— repressed sexuality, the conflict between desire and perceived notions of sin, the dangers of religious fanaticism, the struggle to find truth in a world of expedient lies, and the restlessness of those in search of personal redemption.

In the play, Myra is unhappily married to the much older Jabe, who is dying of cancer. Their marriage is loveless and passionless. She becomes attracted to a poet passing through town named Val, who awakens her sensuality and desire.

They become lovers, much to the dismay of the sexually aggressive Cassandra, who wanted Val for herself, and the sexually repressed Vee, who wears religion like a chastity belt. When Jabe discovers Myra's infidelity, he kills her and frames Val. Fanatical townspeople lynch Val and burn him alive.

The guild chose Boston for the play's pre-Broadway run. In retrospect, it was a curious choice, considering the city's then-noted Catholic conservatism. The play opened December 30, 1940, and was a disaster from the opening curtain. Many Bostonians sat slack-jawed at some of the play's imagery, such as when Vee paints a portrait of Val as a Christ figure.

It was a fitting finale when the prop master overdid the smoke pots during Val's blowtorch death. He filled the theater with thick smoke, choking actors and audience alike, forcing many of those sitting in orchestra seats to leave the theater. When the actors came out for their bows, half the house was empty.

A week later, responding to complaints from a few angry theatergoers, Boston City officials demanded the painting scene be removed from the play, along with other offensive dialogue. Interestingly, critics were thoughtful and generally supportive of Williams's effort. *The Boston Herald's* Alexander Williams wrote, "The scene where the religious fanatic discovers that she has painted [Val] as Christ is uncomfortable, but that is due to our own scruples and the playwright's uncompromising realism."[6]

Words of praise could not save the play. After completing its two-week run in Boston, the guild told Williams they would not mount a New York production. Instead, they gave him an advance to rewrite the play. In February 1941, he received a $500 grant from the Rockefeller Foundation, and after having cataract surgery, he left New York for Key West to work on the play revisions. Upon his return to New York, the guild made it clear they had no interest in reviving the play. He did not handle the disappointment well.

In March 1942, Williams underwent a second eye operation, after which he embarked on a self-destructive binge of overdrinking and promiscuity that lasted for months. Over the next year, he would take a series of menial jobs—elevator operator, movie usher, dishwasher, and waiter. The jobs never lasted long and money was scarce, forcing Williams to frequently depend on the kindness of friends. Through it all, he continued to write, collaborating with his friend Donald Windham on *You Touched Me*, a play inspired by a D. H. Lawrence story.

The spring of 1943 was a sad season. His grandmother was dying of cancer, and Williams traveled back to St. Louis to visit his grandparents, who were now living with Edwina and Cornelius. Most upsetting were the letters from Rose, still institutionalized at Farmington. It was during that visit, while brooding over his sister's letters, that Williams began writing the first draft of a play he called *The Gentleman Caller*. He dedicated the play to Rose and told his close friend Donald Windham it was a personal history of his family.

That May, Audrey Wood came through in a huge way. She had somehow managed to get Tennessee a job at MGM Studios in Los Angeles as a screenwriter. The pay was an astonishing $250 *a week* for a six-month contract. Williams instructed Wood to send much of his salary to his mother to help pay for his grandmother's medical expenses and to pay for Rose to spend the summer at a private rest home.

His first assignment at MGM was a star vehicle for Lana Turner called *Marriage Is a Private Affair*. According to Edwina, "He worked on it for several weeks, then handed in what he believed a good script. The powers-that-be read it and informed him . . . it was not for Lana. I think they meant it was too high-brow.

"He was then asked to write a scenario for a film featuring the child star, Margaret O'Brien. Tom's reply was frank if hardly the height of diplomacy. 'Child stars make me sick.'"[7]

Instead, Williams put together a treatment for a film based on *The Gentleman Caller*. That was not well received, either, and the studio passed. It was obvious that Williams was not a good fit as a screenwriter. MGM dropped him but honored his six-month contract. That allowed Williams to rent a room in Santa Monica overlooking the ocean and work on his play.

Theater producer Margo Jones, known as the Texas Tornado, optioned *You Touched Me* and went to Los Angeles to work with Williams on rewrites. For reasons unknown, Windham was not included—even though the play had originally been his idea. He was understandably upset, particularly when Williams expected him to take less than his agreed-upon 50-50 take of the royalties. It caused a breach in the friendship that never fully healed.

Jones opened the play in Cleveland, then moved it to the Pasadena Playhouse in California. *You Touched Me* would eventually make it to Broadway in 1945 at the Booth Theater, where it received indifferent reviews. It ran for 109 performances, or about three months, before closing.

Shortly after the New Year in 1944, Tennessee learned his grandmother didn't have long to live. He rushed back to St. Louis. On January 6, she died with Tennessee by her bedside. He was so distraught, he couldn't attend the funeral, choosing instead to schedule another eye operation for that very day. This time, doctors were able to correct his sight enough that with the aid of glasses, his left eye would be usable.

He returned to California and grieved through his writing. When he arrived back in New York, he handed Audrey Wood the finished play, which he had renamed *The Glass Menagerie*.

He also learned he was being honored by the National Academy of Arts and Letters for his one-acts, which had quietly been gaining recognition through performances by small theater companies. He was presented with $1,000 and a certificate which read:

To Tennessee Williams, born in Mississippi, in recognition of his dramatic works, which reveal a poetic imagination and a gift for characterization that are rare in the contemporary theatre.[8]

Just how much a gift he had would soon become apparent to everyone who saw *The Glass Menagerie*. What makes the play so haunting is that its themes of loss and family are universally human. It is Williams's most directly autobiographical play, and he channels his forlorn sadness and guilt and helplessness about his sister through Tom Wingfield's final monologue:

I didn't go to the moon, I went much further, but time is the longest distance between two places. I left St. Louis. I descended these steps of the fire escape for the last time . . . trying to find in motion what was lost in space . . .

I would have stopped but I was pursued by something. It always came upon me unawares, taking me altogether by surprise. Perhaps it was a familiar bit of music, perhaps it was only a piece of transparent glass. Perhaps walking along a street at night in some strange city. . . . I passed the lighted window where perfume is sold. The window is filled with pieces of colored glass, tiny, transparent bottles in delicate colors, like bits of a shattered rainbow. Then all at once my sister touches my shoulder. I turn around and look into her eyes. Oh, Laura. Laura, I tried to leave you behind me, but I am more faithful than I intended to be!

I reach for a cigarette. I cross the street. I run into a movie or a bar. I buy a drink. I speak to the nearest stranger—anything that can blow your candles out, for nowadays the world is lit by lightning. Blow out your candles, Laura—and so goodbye.[9]

After six years of wandering and relentless struggle, of financial desperation and agonizing self-doubt, Tennessee Williams had broken through. One of the first things he did was to sign over half the rights of *Menagerie* to his mother, making sure she would always be taken care of—and no longer financially dependent on Cornelius. It was as much a slap at his father as it was a gift to his mother.

"Tom's success was a bitter pill for Cornelius," Edwina acknowledged. "The son he always berated as a failure, whom he taunted as 'Miss Nancy' when he was growing up, because he wasn't an athlete, whom he had pulled out of college when he failed R.O.T.C., was now achieving a financial income far beyond his father's. Life can be beautifully ironic."[10]

Other times, the irony can be maddening. Williams would later describe his life before the success of *The Glass Menagerie* as "one that required endurance, a life of clawing and scratching along a sheer surface and holding on tight with raw fingers."[11] And yet, people tend to become accustomed to their circumstances, however difficult. Now that he was financially secure and touted as one of America's finest playwrights, a different kind of desperation grabbed hold of Williams. Success terrified him—the attention, the pressure to live up to expectations, both his own and others', were new forces he hadn't dealt with before.

He fled New York for Mexico, where he could be the Tennessee of old. There he started work on his next play—one that would ensure his theater legacy.

Margo Jones

Margo Jones (left) with Tennessee Williams (right)

Known as the Texas Tornado, Margaret Virginia Jones was one of the leading forces behind the regional theater movement. Born in Livingston, Texas, on December 12, 1911, Margo was a bit of a prodigy. She graduated from high school when she was just fifteen and entered the Girls' Industrial College of Texas—now Texas Woman's University—where she earned a bachelor of arts degree in speech and, a year later, a master's in psychology and education.

During the summer of 1934, she went to California to study at the Pasadena Playhouse. Founded by Gilmor Brown, who also acted as artistic director, the Playhouse was one of America's first regional theaters. It would gain national prominence for its staging of classical productions as well as new works by contemporary playwrights such as Tennessee Williams.

After a brief association with the Ojai Community Theatre, Margo traveled the world in 1935, watching performances and soaking up whatever she could learn about presenting plays. When she got back to Texas, she was hired by the Houston Federal Theatre Project as assistant director.

Not one to waste time, Margo founded her own local theater company, the Houston Community Players, in 1936. She was recognized in 1939 by *Stage* magazine as one of the twelve outstanding theater directors outside of New York—and the only woman named.

In 1942 she stepped down as the Houston Community Players' artistic director and for the next two years taught theater and directed plays at the University of Texas. That same year she met Tennessee Williams and staged two of his early plays, *You Touched Me* and *The Purification*, at the Pasadena Playhouse.

Around that time she developed an idea for a network of nonprofit professional regional theaters. She applied for a Rockefeller Fellowship to help fund it, but her project was interrupted when she was asked to codirect *The Glass Menagerie*. Because of that show's success, Jones had the juice she needed to establish the first nonprofit resident theater, located in Dallas.

The theater, which opened in 1947, was the first professional theater-in-the-round as well as the first nonprofit professional resident theater. Over the next eight years, Jones produced eighty-five plays, including *Summer and Smoke*, and Inge's *The Dark at the Top of the Stairs* in the theater's inaugural season. When Jerome Lawrence and Robert E. Lee could not find any New York producers willing to stage *Inherit the Wind*—a fictionalized account of the Scopes Monkey Trial—out of concern it was too controversial, Jones produced it in Dallas. After the show opened to rave reviews, Harold Shumlin brought it to Broadway, with Jones as associate producer.

Although she staged classics, Jones's passion was discovering and nurturing new talent. She never apologized for her own Broadway ambitions, but Jones was aware that the commercialism of Broadway needed to be balanced or else up-and-coming writers would find it increasingly difficult to develop and hone their craft. Socially aware, she supported diversity and helped organize the African-American amateur Round-up Theatre company.

When she wasn't staging new productions, Jones was helping other communities establish their own resident theaters, laying the foundation for the regional theater movement, which she would not live to see. Jones died July 24, 1955, after inhaling carbon tetrachloride fumes; the chemical had been used to clean the carpets in her apartment. The theater world was stunned. Her theater never recovered—it closed four years after her death—but her legacy continues to live on.

Today there are over 300 resident nonprofit theaters in communities across America. They produce innovative works and groom the next generation of playwrights, directors, and actors. New York producers regularly scout these theaters, looking for the next great Broadway show.

For her contribution to the arts, the Texas Historical Commission declared Jones's birthplace a state landmark.

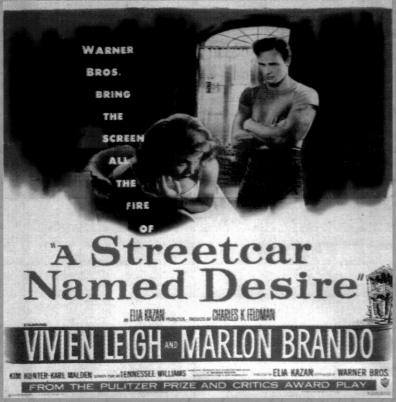

A Streetcar Named Desire added to Williams' growing reputation as an important new playwright. The play would become his most successful and, like *The Glass Menagerie*, would be made into a movie. The Broadway production, which premiered in March 1947, starred a then-unknown twenty-three-year-old Marlon Brando as Stanley Kowalski.

Chapter 7

Brutal Desire

Now that he had money, Williams began to wander on a Ulysses-like scale. For over a year following *The Glass Menagerie*'s Broadway debut, Williams hopscotched across North America—Mexico, New Orleans, Dallas, Chicago, Key West, Nantucket, Taos. . . . His agent seldom knew where to reach her client except when he was passing through New York and stopped by the office to check in. It's as if he needed to be in perpetual motion to protect his muse from the evils of success. He reflected:

> Once you know . . . that the heart of man, his body and his brain, are forged in a white-hot furnace for the purpose of conflict . . . that not privation but luxury is the wolf at the door and that the fangs of this wolf are all the little vanities and conceits and laxities that Success is heir to . . . you are at least in a position of knowing where the danger lies.
>
> The public Somebody you are when you *have a name* is a fiction created with mirrors and that the only somebody worth being is the solitary and unseen you that existed from your first breath and which is the sum of your actions . . . knowing these things, you can even survive the catastrophe of Success![1]

While spending the summer of 1946 in Nantucket, Williams developed an unusual friendship with author Carson McCullers. After reading *The Member of the Wedding*, Williams arranged through mutual friends to meet the eccentric Georgia writer, who ended up spending much of the summer at Williams's rented house. They shared stories, read and discussed the poetry of Hart Crane, and shared the same table for their daily writing sessions.

Her company inspired him and he completed the first draft of a new play, eventually known as *Summer and Smoke*, which examined a woman's struggle to express her repressed erotic desires. Set in 1910 Mississippi, Alma Winemiller is a minister's daughter in love with a young doctor. She flirts, but when he makes advances, she backs away, too inhibited to follow through. By the time she builds the courage to accept the doctor's proposition, he rejects her, having found someone else. Devastated, she sheds the inhibitions of her upbringing and, at least for one night, impulsively goes off with a traveling salesman she meets at the park in an effort to balance her needs of the flesh with spiritual purity.

The conflict between religion and basic human needs—guilt/desire, lust/love, honesty/delusion—would become a recurring theme in Williams's work. "Some people cling to a certain philosophy that is handed down to them and which they accept," he once observed. "Life has a meaning if you're bucking for heaven. But if heaven is a fantasy, we are in this jungle with whatever we can work out for ourselves. It seems to me that the cards are stacked against us."[2] That sense of hopelessness was never more forcefully expressed than in his next play, a Southern Gothic masterpiece.

When he had been in Chicago for *Menagerie*'s rehearsals, Tennessee started writing a draft for *Blanche's Chair in the Moon*. When he escaped to Mexico after *Menagerie*'s success in New York, he resumed dabbling with the play, now titled *The Poker Night*. While he had outlined some individual scenes, he still didn't have a narrative to connect them, so he put the play aside until the autumn of 1946, when the characters finally came to life in his head.

Years later, he would explain, "My characters make my play. I always start with them; they take spirit and body in my mind. Nothing that they say or do is arbitrary or invented. They build the play around them like spiders weaving their webs, sea creatures making their shells. I live with them for a year and a half or two years and I know them far better than I know myself, since I created them and not myself."[3]

In March 1947, Williams sent *The Poker Night* to his agent. Within two months, Irene Mayer Selznick—who was the daughter of MGM cofounder Louis B. Mayer and married to *Gone With the Wind* producer David O. Selznick—agreed to produce the play. Williams had renamed it again, calling it *A Streetcar Named Desire*.

Set during a steamy New Orleans summer, Blanche DuBois comes to stay with her younger sister Stella, who is pregnant with her first child. Although they had grown up Southern aristocrats on their parents' Mississippi plantation, Belle Reve, Stella has found happiness with her genuinely adoring husband Stanley Kowalski, a mechanic who is as unrefined as he is sensual. They share an intense sexual passion that Blanche claims to find as distasteful as their cramped apartment. She also considers Stanley crude and dangerous. At the same time, she is attracted to his brutish animal magnetism.

Blanche has come to New Orleans because the family money is long gone and the estate has been taken for back taxes. Stanley immediately perceives Blanche as a threat to his marriage, and soon it becomes a contest of wills for Stella's loyalty. It is also a clash between the dying genteel, Old South and the harsh world of the industrial working class.

One night Stanley holds a poker game with some friends, and Blanche catches the eye of Mitch, a gentle man who cares for his ailing mother. She goes out of her way to charm Mitch, desperate for affection and to find someone to take care of her. She tells Mitch she is on a leave of absence from her job as a high school teacher and presents herself as a chaste, traditional Southern lady. She also confesses she was once married and discovered her young husband was homosexual after she walked in on him with an older man. She reacted with cruel words and he committed suicide, leaving her alone. Fearing for his own loneliness, Mitch proposes.

Meanwhile, Stanley finds out that Blanche is not what she presents herself to be. He tells Stella and Mitch the truth. She was fired from her teaching job for having an affair with one of her students. After losing Belle Reve, she moved into a local hotel and turned to prostituting herself to survive. She was eventually asked to leave and was practically run out of town. Homeless and penniless, she had no choice but to seek shelter with her sister.

Later, Blanche can't figure out why Mitch hasn't shown up—it's her birthday and they were supposed to celebrate together. Stanley hands her a present—a one-way ticket back to Mississippi—and she understands what has happened. Their ensuing argument is interrupted when Stella goes into labor.

Alone, Blanche gets drunk and Mitch shows up to confront her. She eventually admits to her past and that after her husband's suicide she can only find comfort—however temporary—through sexual encounters with strangers.

"I stayed at a hotel called the Tarantula Arms. . . . Yes, a big spider. That's where I brought my victims. Yes, I have had many meetings with strangers. After the death of Allan, meetings with strangers was all I seemed able to fill my empty heart with. I think it was panic, just panic, that drove me from one to another searching for some protection. Here, there, and then in the most unlikely places."[4]

Mitch roughly demands sex but Blanche demands marriage first. When Mitch tells her she's not clean enough to be in the same house with his mother, she forces him out.

Stanley comes home from the hospital to find Blanche teetering on the emotional edge. He taunts her about her lies, but Blanche claims she is only trying to add beauty to an otherwise ugly existence. "I don't want realism. I want magic! I do misrepresent things. I don't tell the truth. I tell what *ought* to be truth."[5]

Stanley had been drinking to celebrate his pending fatherhood, and the liquor is fueling his animosity toward Blanche and his disgust over her previous flirting. Their verbal confrontation becomes violently physical and he rapes her.

Several days later, Stella is back home and Blanche's bags are packed. Stella has refused to believe that Stanley assaulted Blanche, choosing her husband over her sister. A doctor shows up to take an emotionally shattered Blanche to a mental hospital. At first fearful, she finally goes with the doctor, explaining, "Whoever you are, I have always depended on the kindness of strangers."[6]

Selznick and Williams agreed that Elia Kazan, who had followed Williams's career via his wife, Molly Day Thacher, would be the perfect director. While preproduction for *Streetcar* began in New York, Margo Jones was staging a pre-Broadway run of *Summer and Smoke* in Dallas. Williams decided to celebrate by spending the month of June 1947 in Provincetown, Rhode Island, with Jones and his companion, Pancho Rodriguez.

While there, Tennessee got a telegram from Kazan, "informing me that he was dispatching a young actor he thought was gifted and wanted him to read the part of Stanley. We waited two or three days but the young actor, named Marlon Brando, didn't show. I had stopped expecting him when he arrived one evening with a young girl."[7]

When he read, there was no doubt in his or Jones's mind that the twenty-three-year-old Brando *was* Stanley Kowalski. "I never saw such raw talent in an individual," Williams later said. "Brando was a gentle, lovely guy, a man of extraordinary beauty."[8]

A Streetcar Named Desire premiered December 3, 1947, at the Ethel Barrymore Theatre to glowing reviews. It would be his most successful play, winning the New York Drama Critics Circle Award and a Pulitzer Prize for drama. (Williams gave the prize money to the University of Missouri for a graduate journalism scholarship.) Not only did the play advance theater, the characters of Blanche and Stanley became cultural icons and generated debate and discussion that continues still.

In discussing Blanche, director Elia Kazan believed her inability to overcome her traditional upbringing is her fatal flaw. "She won't face her physical or sensual side. She calls it *brutal desire*. She thinks she sins when she gives in to it . . . yet she does give in to it, out of loneliness . . . but by calling it *brutal desire,* she is able to separate it from her *real self,* her cultured, refined self. Her tradition makes no allowance, allows no space for this very part of herself so she is constantly in conflict."[9]

Williams said Stanley's violence against Blanche is "activated more by misunderstanding than malice; a blindness to what is going on in each other's hearts. Stanley sees Blanche not as a desperate, driven creature backed into a last corner to make a last desperate stand—but as a calculating bitch with 'round heels.' . . . Nobody sees anybody truly but all through the flaws of their own egos."[10]

The success of *Streetcar* once again sent Williams running from the limelight. This time he hopped a steamship to Europe for an extended vacation, looking forward to the solitude of traveling alone.

Southern Gothic

Ellen Glasgow

In 1936, future Pulitzer Prize–winning novelist Ellen Glasgow was speaking at the University of Virginia before a gathering of librarians. Glasgow, who gained fame writing books typically set in her native Virginia, was discussing a new trend in Southern literature that she called Southern Gothic.

What she specifically meant has been open to interpretation, but today Southern Gothic refers to fiction characterized by Southern settings; dark or haunting situations that often deal with taboo subjects such as incest, rape, or madness; and mysterious, desolate, or grotesque characters that are remnants—or victims—of the region's traditional social conventions. The genre exploits Gothic elements to provide emotional context of the culture unique to the American South.

According to Ann B. Tracy's *The Gothic Novel*, "The world of Gothic fiction is characterized by a chronic sense of apprehension and the premonition of impending but unidentified disaster. The Gothic world is the fallen world, the vision of fallen man, living in fear and alienation . . . Gothic heroes and heroines are on their own, stumbling alone . . . through appalling complexities of decision and action, obliged to find their own solutions or go under; estrangement from family ties is their normal condition."[11]

The Gothic style has long been a fixture in novels, a form of literature that matured in the eighteenth century as a reaction to the popularity of romanticism. Many novelists in that era took inspiration for their stories from the so-called romantic traditions—oral legends, myths, and stories passed down through the ages. These novels were also often set in the past and were typically filled with a kind of grandeur. It was the literary equivalent of Hollywood's sweeping Technicolor melodramas like *Gone with the Wind*.

The writers most often associated with Southern Gothic are William Faulkner, Carson McCullers, Tennessee Williams, Flannery O'Connor, and Truman Capote. Many of the works by these writers share common themes, such as the isolation experienced by their characters, whether through physical disability (Laura in *Glass Menagerie*) or simply having a unique personal perspective. Characters often experience some form of imprisonment, sometimes literal but more likely figurative. In Williams's *The Rose Tattoo*, Serafina has imprisoned her heart out of a misguided sense of loyalty toward her dead husband. Southern Gothic also tends to be emotionally and often physically violent, such as Stanley's rape of Blanche.

Perhaps the most notable aspect of Southern Gothic is the sense of place it evokes, with strong, almost visceral images that reek of the passions and emotions of the characters and their struggles. Nobody would ever mistake the atmosphere in *Streetcar* with Chicago or Los Angeles; *Summer and Smoke* would not play out in Minnesota in quite the same lusty way.

Typically, Tennessee Williams stretched the bounds of Southern Gothic—particularly in his one-acts—infusing his work with a clear-eyed lyricism that gave the genre new power to pointedly refute lingering stereotypes. He wasn't interested in creating suspense; he used Gothic elements to explore societal and cultural transformations. The decaying Old South was symbolic of those forces (tradition, religion) that prevent people from being true to their nature.

The protagonists in Williams's work are anti-heroes with glaring flaws who become relatable to the audience because of their innate humanness. Through these characters, Williams was able to lay bare the hypocrisies he saw in Southern culture, as well as the affection he had for it—something often overlooked. His mother recalled how he addressd this criticism:

> I assure you that the South is the country of my heart as well as my birth. . . . My childhood was spent in the South and childhood is always the magic part of life. In the South there's a greater sense of honor, of decency . . . though it disturbs me to find the South so conservative in its social point of view.
>
> I don't think of my . . . people as damned—not as long as they keep courage and gallantry. Those are important and very Southern qualities, bred in the bones of the people I wrote about, such as Amanda Wingfield . . . .
>
> I write out of love for the South. But I can't expect Southerners to realize that my writing about them is an expression of love. It is out of a regret for a South that no longer exists that I write of the forces that have destroyed it.[12]

His theatrical success allowed Williams the financial freedom to travel. A nomad at heart, he seemed constantly
on the move. Part of his restlessness stemmed from
his belief that geographical environment affected his
writing, so he was always searching for places that stirred
his creativity. After the success of *Streetcar*, Williams
traveled to Europe, sailing on the *Queen Mary*.

Chapter 8

"The Little Horse"

Williams's extended 1948 vacation in Europe did little to quell his inner demons. He found Paris dreary and took to cruising known pickup areas late at night, indiscriminately taking young men back to his hotel. At least once he was robbed by an overnight companion. Still, he was unable to control his seeming compulsion for anonymous, emotionless sexual trysts.

After Paris he went to Rome, where he finished revisions for the Broadway debut of *Summer and Smoke* later that year. And with that, he took a prolonged break from writing for the first time since he was eleven. Without his characters to distract him, without stories to engage him, without that emotional outlet to comfort him, Tennessee Williams's normal self-indulgences became self-destructive. He started taking pills to heighten the effects of his drinking. Getting stoned dulled Williams's overactive libido, and some friends quietly speculated he was simply exchanging one risky behavior for a different, more potentially lethal addiction.

The first sign he was developing a problem was at the London premiere of *The Glass Menagerie* in the summer of 1948. His mother and brother had traveled to London for the gala opening at the Theatre Royal Haymarket on July 28, as had Audrey Wood. Williams's scheduled arrival time came and went with no sign of the playwright. He was also AWOL for the performance.

Among the people puzzled by his absence was Maria Britneva, a mid-level actress who had met Williams a month earlier at a party thrown by John Gielgud, who was directing the London staging of *Glass Menagerie*. The two hit it off immediately upon discovering they both had been raised by their grandmothers (which might have been news to Edwina). It was the beginning of a friendship that would endure for thirty years—and one that few people were even aware of. Maria, who later married a British aristocrat and became Lady Maria St. Just, became his most trusted confidante. They exchanged hundreds of letters over the course of their unique relationship. Because Williams tended to write Maria's letters after he finished his day's work, he called her his "five o'clock angel."

Maria, who attended the premiere with theatrical producers John Perry and Hugh "Binkie" Beaumont, introduced herself to Edwina and, according to the book *Five O'Clock Angel*, said, "Mrs. Williams was a tiny little woman. Nobody dared ask her where her famous son was. John, Binkie and I were left to entertain her. She remained very dignified throughout Tennessee's disappearance."[1]

At the sumptuous reception that followed, Edwina received a telegram from her wayward son, who was still in Paris, telling her to take a bow for him. Edwina was not remotely amused, and Wood was mortified that her client had stood up the cast and director. Williams later wrote directly to Helen Hayes, who was starring as Amanda, and apologized for what he termed his childish behavior. According to biographer Donald Spoto, "Williams . . . explained his rudeness by detailing a condition of exhaustion, overwork, frayed nerves, emotional paralysis and—Alma Winemiller's complaint—heart palpitations. His failure to arrive, he wrote, was due to an accidental overdose of the sedative barbital he had taken to quiet a nerve crisis; he then fell unconscious for five hours and missed his train."[2]

Hayes seemed mollified, but Williams's use of pills concerned Audrey Wood. Tennessee had been a lifelong hypochondriac, dramatically claiming dire illness and imminent death over the slightest of ailments—which coincided with times of stress or depression. His exaggerations were taken in stride by those who knew him best, but for Wood, the idea that he was self-medicating was deeply disturbing.

In October 1948, Williams returned to New York for the opening of *Summer and Smoke*. While walking down Fifty-eighth Street one evening, he glanced into a deli and spotted Frank Merlo, a handsome young man with whom he had shared a brief encounter in Provincetown the year before. There had been an immediate attraction and strong personal connection between them, but at the time, Tennessee had been involved with Pancho. He had also been crazed with the preproduction of *Streetcar*. Merlo had moved on.

That night they resumed their relationship. Williams was initially wary of getting *too* involved, having become used to the freedom of being single. However, during a trip back to St. Louis, he realized he finally wanted to commit to someone. "It became unmistakably clear to me that my heart, too long accustomed to transitory attachments, had found in the young Sicilian a home at last."[3]

Williams finally had a true partner, whom he affectionately called the Little Horse. "We were all very pleased when Frank moved in with Tenn," Paul Bigelow recalled to Donald Spoto. "Frank was a warm, decent man with a strong native intelligence and a sense of honor. Those of us who cared about Tenn realized that Frank wanted to care for him and provide some order in his chaotic life. . . . And with great love, this is what Frank did."[4]

Artist Christopher Isherwood echoed Bigelow's appreciation of Merlo, calling him "a marvelous man. He ran the house, he looked after him in a way that was uncanny. He was no goody-goody. He was just plain good. And it wasn't some kind of faithful servitor. He was a lovable man with a strong will . . . he was a man who kept his cool, even when he and Tennessee were exposed to the most appalling pressures of social and professional life."[5]

In November, Williams went to St. Louis and, for the first time in a decade, visited Rose at Farmington. As he had previously done for his mother, Williams now made sure his sister was financially secure. He had Dakin, who was by now a practicing attorney, draw up the necessary papers so that half the royalties from *Summer and Smoke* would go to Rose. While there, Williams started the first draft of what would evolve into *Sweet Bird of Youth*.

The house was now a peaceful place to work because Cornelius no longer lived there—just Edwina and her father. During one of the Reverend's extended trips to visit Tom, Cornelius had informed Edwina she couldn't invite him back. Incensed that Cornelius would put her nonagenarian father out on the street, she refused and told Cornelius if he didn't like it he could leave. He did.

Rather than go to court for everything she would be entitled to in a divorce, she requested the house. Cornelius complied and went to live with his sister for a while. He then settled back in St. Louis at a hotel near the family house.

"I never saw Cornelius again after he left Arundel Place," Edwina said in her memoirs. "I was happy to have my freedom—the walls of the house had resounded with wrath for too many years and now there was peace at long last."[6]

In 1949, Williams and Merlo went to Los Angeles, where Warner Brothers was filming the movie adaptation of *The Glass Menagerie*. Williams was annoyed at the "Hollywoodization" of his play, specifically the decision to add a new, more upbeat ending. When the Motion Picture Association of America's censor department insisted a bathroom be changed into a lounge so that a toilet fixture would not be shown on screen, Tennessee had had enough. He and Frank went to St. Louis to pick up his grandfather and headed to Key West, where Williams had rented a house for six months. These were perhaps the most domestic months of his life.

Bigelow told Spoto that Williams stayed there so long because "his grandfather loved it there. It was his refuge from St. Louis and Frank saw to it that [Reverend Dakin] was treated with deference by one and all and that no comfort was lacking. There was a homey atmosphere in Key West. Tenn wrote each day at one end of the dining room table, Frank cooked and ran the house, the Reverend was a respectable addition to the household—it was all very much a family."[7]

Having been underwhelmed with Hollywood's handling of *Menagerie*, Williams had higher hopes for *Streetcar*, because it was to be directed by Elia Kazan, who he felt would stay true to the emotions and spirit of the play. The fact that Warner Brothers had paid him half a million dollars for the rights also helped improve his outlook—in part because the windfall allowed him move Rose out of the state mental hospital at Farmington and into a private hospital in Ossining, New York.

Producer Cheryl Crawford, who cofounded the Actors Studio with Elia Kazan and Robert Lewis, recalled going to visit Rose with Williams. "I always felt he had an enormous guilt about Rose," she told Donald Spoto, "that he'd done nothing to stop the lobotomy and that he felt responsible for the emptiness in her life. There was no question . . . of his devotion to her. It was very touching to see them together."[8]

His work continued to be filled with imagery relating to his sister, sometimes subtly, other times overtly, as in *The Rose Tattoo*, which had debuted at the Martin Beck Theatre on February 3, 1950. Earthy and sexy, the play is also a kind of love poem to Merlo.

Serafina Delle Rose is a widow living on the Gulf Coast, grieving the death of her husband. The rose in the play's title refers to a tattoo he had on his chest, which she saw as a symbol of their love. To honor their relationship and hold on to the sanitized memory of her not-so-faithful husband, Serafina avoids love—and, by extension, life. When a truck driver falls in love with her, it forces Serafina to finally let go of her denials so that she can once again be open to love.

Deborah La Vine, who directed a staging of the play at L.A.'s Hudson Theatre, discussed the complexities of the play with the *Daily Bruin*. Not only does it deal with the fear of getting close to someone and opening up to them, "It is about how love rejuvenates us all and it's the ultimate need for the human soul. This play is absolutely about how the search for love can consume you. . . . Blooming and the sense of opening up, the peeling open of the heart is beautifully personified by the image like the rose."[9]

The Rose Tattoo won the Tony for Best Play, Williams's first and last. It was also the only one of his major plays that had a distinctly happy ending. Tennessee's optimism would prove to be unsustainable.

Christopher Isherwood

Christopher Isherwood

Like the work of Tennessee Williams, Christopher Isherwood's writing is largely autobiographical. However, where Williams's plays tend to be intensely lyrical and filled with allegory, Christopher Isherwood's best fiction is rooted in a gritty realism.

Isherwood was born August 26, 1904, in Cheshire, England, the son of a career army officer who would later be killed in World War I. When he was ten, Christopher was sent to St. Edmund's preparatory school. There he met fellow student Wystan Auden, a budding poet who would later be known as W. H. Auden. They quickly developed a close friendship that would last the rest of their lives—but the rest of his school experience left Isherwood cold.

In *Lions and Shadows*, he recounted his less-than-enthusiastic attendance at the Repton School—the equivalent of a high school boarding school. "I had arrived . . . thoroughly sick of masters and mistresses, having been emotionally messed about by them at my preparatory school, where the war years had given full license to every sort of dishonest cant about loyalty, selfishness, patriotism, playing the game and dishonoring the dead."[10]

He attended college at Corpus Christie Cambridge but didn't stay long enough to earn a degree. He got a job as a personal secretary to a violinist and made extra money as a tutor. His first novel, *All the Conspirators*, was published in 1928, when he was just twenty-four years old.

Although personally comfortable with his homosexuality, Isherwood felt repressed in his family's upper-class society. In 1930, he traveled to Berlin, Germany, which was then known for its tolerance to gay lifestyles. While there, he supported himself by teaching English. After soaking in the atmosphere of 1930s Berlin, he returned to England in 1933.

Two years later he wrote the first of two books about his experiences in Berlin, *Mr. Norris Changes Trains*. In 1939, a collection of short stories, *Goodbye to Berlin,* was published. It possessed a tremendously vivid sense of place as Isherwood introduced the reader to the sometimes decadent excesses of Berlin and the city's eccentric characters, including Sally Bowles, the quintessential individualistic free spirit.

Goodbye to Berlin was also a powerful—and disturbing—depiction of pre-Hitler Germany sliding toward Nazi control. The seeds of anti-Semitism and national jingoism were already blooming into the madness that would result in the atrocities of World War II.

After a trip to China, Isherwood and Auden moved to the United States in 1939. They settled in Los Angeles, where Isherwood worked as a movie studio screenwriter and was introduced to Hinduism.

In 1946 Isherwood became an American citizen. That same year, *Goodbye to Berlin* and *Mr. Norris Changes Trains* were combined into *The Berlin Stories*. Several years later, Isherwood agreed to have the book adapted for the stage by John Van Druten. The result was the critically acclaimed *I Am a Camera*, the title taken from one of the short stories in *Goodbye to Berlin*: "I am a camera with its shutter open, quite passive, recording, not thinking. Recording the man shaving at the window opposite and the woman in the kimono washing her hair. Some day, all this will have to be developed, carefully printed, fixed."[11] *I Am a Camera* was later the basis for the stage musical *Cabaret*.

In 1953 Isherwood met an eighteen-year-old aspiring artist named Don Bachardy, who became his life partner. Like Williams, Isherwood lived openly among friends and associates, but he did not publicly acknowledge being gay until his 1976 autobiography *With Christopher and His Kind*. In the book, an honest recounting of his early life, he explains the importance of his sexual orientation to his work.

Isherwood became one of the first internationally known figures to come out. From that point on, he became an outspoken gay rights activist.

Isherwood died on January 4, 1986, in Santa Monica, California, at the age of eighty-two. Don Bachardy was at his side.

The success of *Cat on a Hot Tin Roof* cemented Williams's place as one of America's greatest dramatists. The play earned Tennessee a second Pulitzer Prize for playwriting. It also earned a Drama Critics' Circle Award for Best New American Play, which was presented by drama critic Walter Kerr (right) at a benefit performance at the Morosco Theatre, New York City.

Chapter 9

Mendacity

Williams and Merlo were vacationing in Rome during the summer of 1950 when the advance copies for Tennessee's first novel were issued. Called *The Roman Spring of Mrs. Stone*, it had been written two years earlier, when Williams was finding comfort through casual promiscuity and worrying about the ultimate effects of such a lifestyle on his soul.

In the book, Karen Stone is a recently widowed actress who moves to Rome and fills the emptiness of her life with a desperate effort to recapture her youth through involvement with Paolo, a handsome young gigolo—a man who is paid to be a woman's companion. She falls in love but in the end is used by Paolo, who leaves. She then hooks up with another young man to keep her company.

Transparently autobiographical, the novel prompted Donald Windham to write in his memoirs that the book was Tennessee's "first fictionalized self-portrait after his success—and it displays a hair-raising degree of self-knowledge."[1]

Williams and Merlo returned to the United States in the autumn for the opening of *The Rose Tattoo,* but by the following May, Williams was ready to take another extended trip abroad. His nomadic nature required sacrifice from Merlo, who would have been happy to make Key West their permanent residence.

Williams's next original Broadway production, the highly experimental *Camino Real,* was a critical flop and an emotional disaster for Williams. After a string of successes, the failure he'd feared had materialized. The complex, metaphorical play, with obvious political undertones and filled with historical characters trapped in a netherworld, left audiences confused and had critics filing their verbal claws. Reviewer Walter Kerr sniped, it was "the worst play yet written by the best playwright of this generation."[2]

There was possibly another reason for the harsh critical backlash. Many saw the play as an over-the-top indictment against the paranoiac rhetoric of Senator Joseph McCarthy, who spearheaded a political witch hunt against anyone suspected of having Communist sympathies.

In the Williams biography *The Kindness of Strangers*, actress Barbara Baxley recalled, "The earlier version of the play was an unwaveringly, anti-imperialist play. It certainly was not anti-American, however—it was anti-fascist. But all references in the play to fascism in America, and to brotherhood and love were cut, since they were thought to be ringing cries of Communist sympathy."[3]

Williams immediately left New York and holed up in Key West. He revised the play for its published version and added a calm, thoughtful afterword that probably belied his inner turmoil: "The printed script of a play is hardly more than an architect's blueprint of a house not yet built or built and destroyed. The color, the grace and levitation, the structural pattern in motion, the quick interplay of live beings, suspended like fitful lightning in a cloud, these things are the play, not words on paper, nor thoughts and ideas of an author."[4]

In 1953, Williams left yet again for an extended European vacation. Years later, director Richard Seyd would observe that rather than spur his creativity the way adventures and excursions had earlier in his career, Williams's wanderings at this point would ultimately prove to have the opposite effect. "He had to flee the country, and the country was the source of his artistry, the culture in which he grew up was the source . . . ," Seyd remarked. "I think the hardest thing about being an artist and a celebrity is that you lose your connection to the source because people are watching you, rather than you being able to watch people. . . . It's true for an actor, and in Tennessee's case . . . true for him as a writer."[5]

In early 1954, Williams began work on a play inspired by his own short story "Three Players of a Summer Game." By the end of the year he gave Audrey Wood the completed draft of *Cat on a Hot Tin Roof*, about a dysfunctional family whose members are forced to confront their hypocrisy and mendacity.

The play takes place the night of Big Daddy Pollitt's sixty-fifth birthday celebration at the family plantation. He has just been told by his doctor, at the request of the family, that a recent medical condition is simply a spastic colon. In truth, Big Daddy is dying of cancer.

Gooper Pollitt and his wife, Mae, are fearful that Big Daddy will leave the bulk of his wealth and land to his younger brother Brick, who has always been the father's favorite. Mae never misses an opportunity to remind Big Daddy that she and Gooper have already given him and Big Mama grandkids, in hopes of swaying Big Daddy.

The truth Big Daddy has concealed is that he's never cared for his grand-children or Mae or Gooper or even his wife. It was a lie he had to tell and live all these years.

Brick's beautiful, wildly sensual wife, Maggie, is aware of her sister-in-law's scheme and is furious that Brick ignores his brother's blatant attempts to gain control of Big Daddy's fortune. She tries to seduce her husband into making love so that she can get pregnant. However, he refuses to have any physical contact with her at all.

Brick is despondent over the suicide of his best friend Skipper, and seems content to live the rest of his life in a drunken stupor in an effort to dull his guilt—when an emotionally fragile Skipper called to say he wanted to kill himself, Brick had hung up on him. In a pivotal scene, Big Daddy confronts Brick about his drinking and forces him to examine his feelings for Skipper, a love, Maggie notes, that dare not speak its name.

It is ironic that Big Daddy is more accepting of Brick's possible homosexuality than his son can be about it. He also sees Brick's rejection of Skipper as the ultimate betrayal. The question of whether his love for Skipper was indeed simply deep friendship or forged from repressed homoerotic desires is never fully answered. However, Brick's horror at the thought of being outed and publicly scorned for it is certainly implied.

In an attempt to protect her husband, Maggie announces she is pregnant. Of course, it's a lie, but Brick is still surprised and touched by Maggie's loyalty. As the play ends, she finally convinces Brick to make love to her so that she can make good on her lie.

Elia Kazan was chosen to direct the play. Initially Williams wasn't on the same planet when it came to casting. Kazan hired Barbara Bel Geddes, who would become best known as Miss Ellie Ewing on the late-1970s TV series *Dallas*, as Maggie. Burl Ives was cast as Big Daddy, to which a bemused Williams commented, "He's a singer, isn't he?"[6]

However, the casting proved inspired. The play opened March 24, 1955, at the Morosco Theatre and was hailed as his best work since *Streetcar*. It also brought criticism of a different kind—that of mendacity on the part of the playwright for not directly confronting the issue of homosexuality. The *New York Herald Tribune* theater critic, Walter Kerr, accused Williams of being evasive, and *New York* magazine's Eric Bentley chided him for being vague.

For his part, Williams always maintained the primary point of the play was deception and dishonesty—not Brick's ambiguous sexual preference. However, it must be remembered that in 1955, although Williams had long lived openly among friends and associates, the public at large was not aware he was gay. In the highly repressed Eisenhower era of the 1950s, such matters were still not openly discussed. Unlike the information age of today, celebrities of all types lived more private lives, seldom worrying about being outed by the media. It would be another fifteen years before Williams would publicly discuss his homosexuality.

Cat on a Hot Tin Roof propelled Williams back to the top, winning a Drama Critics' Circle Award and a second Pulitzer. The success was bittersweet. A month before the opening, Reverend Dakin died at the age of ninety-seven. Williams lost the one true father figure he'd ever known.

In the summer of 1955, Williams left on another European holiday—alone. Merlo admitted to Audrey Wood that there was trouble in the relationship and they agreed a brief separation might be beneficial to both. Williams's restlessness had never been greater, and he moved from hotel to hotel, country to country, on whims. Margo Jones had been dead two weeks before Williams could be tracked down and told.

It was the first of many separations that increased in frequency and length, and although Williams and Merlo remained attached to one another emotionally, a subtle but unbridgeable distance now yawned between them. It was during this first separation that Williams suffered a serious writing block. He began to take a barbiturate, Seconal, with a martini chaser to spur his creative juices. He would later admit from that point forward, he seldom wrote—or got through the day—without the aid of drugs again.

On March 27, 1957, Dakin called Tennessee to tell him their father had died in a hotel room, alone. Reassessing his father with the hindsight of his own life experience, Williams no longer harbored animosity. Edwina included Tom's remembrance of his father in her memoirs:

> His was not a nature that could comply with the accepted social molds and patterns without a restlessness that would have driven him mad without the release of liquor and poker and wild week-ends. . . . Actually he lived a rather pathetically regular life all week, arriving punctually for a six o'clock dinner, hauling off to bed before midnight and rising at six every morning. There was no charm wasted on the family, to be sure, but I never saw him strike Mother other than verbally, and Mother was a worthy adversary in verbal combat, rarely if ever bested. It was just a wrong marriage, as wrong as a marriage could be, and never should have happened to a dog, let alone two desperate human beings, and their bewildered children.[7]

Williams added later to the *New York Post,* "He lived on his own terms which were hard terms for his family but he should not be judged as long as he remains the mystery that he is to us who lived in his shadow. Maybe I hated him once but I certainly don't anymore."[8]

Later that year, Williams started therapy with Dr. Lawrence Kubie, who promptly told Tennessee he needed to stop writing. Williams surprised everyone, none more so than Dr. Kubie, by doing a television interview with Mike Wallace and disclosing the advice his psychiatrist had been giving him. The revelation prompted Dr. Kubie to ask Williams to find a new therapist—and led to Kubie's losing many patients.

After that, Williams sat down and wrote the allegorical but painfully autobiographical *Suddenly Last Summer,* which was a stark examination of his innermost demons. It also signaled the beginning of his personal and professional downward spiral.

Elia Kazan

In 1999, the Academy of Motion Pictures Arts and Sciences voted to present its Lifetime Achievement Award to Elia Kazan. The announcement provoked a firestorm of controversy and reopened an old wound on the American psyche that had never fully healed.

In 1938, the House of Representatives formed the House Un-American Activities Committee, known as HUAC, to investigate and ferret out subversive organizations operating in the United States. Their prime target was the Communist Party of America, which had formed after World War I.

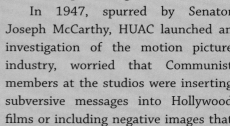

Elia Kazan

HUAC wielded great power and turned American jurisprudence on its ear. Anyone implicated in being disloyal to America was presumed guilty and had to prove their innocence. One way to do that was by naming other individuals who may or may not be disloyal. Anyone refusing to answer questions was cited for Contempt of Congress.

In 1947, spurred by Senator Joseph McCarthy, HUAC launched an investigation of the motion picture industry, worried that Communist members at the studios were inserting subversive messages into Hollywood films or including negative images that would reflect badly on America when the films were released internationally.

During the first round of hearings, HUAC questioned forty-one members of the film industry considered "friendly witnesses." Out of those interviews, HUAC compiled a list of nineteen people accused of holding "left-wing" views.

When the first subpoenas went out, the Motion Picture Association of America (MPAA) denounced the action of HUAC. However, after the first group of screenwriters called to testify instead read statements condemning the committee's actions and were cited for contempt, Hollywood blinked. Fearing bad press and not wanting to take on the federal government, MPAA announced that "no Communists or other subversives will be employed by Hollywood."

The movie industry had officially established a blacklist.

The screenwriters, now known as the Hollywood Ten, were sentenced to a year in jail for contempt and were the first names on the blacklist—all for simply refusing to accuse others. It wasn't just a matter of naming people who had openly expressed communist views; HUAC wanted people who *might* hold left-wing views or who *might* be, or *might* have been, sympathetic to communists. No proof was needed, just innuendo.

Even though it was film-career suicide, hundreds of people refused to comply with HUAC. The blacklist grew to over 300 names, including Stella Adler, Charlie Chaplin, Dashiell Hammett, Burl Ives, Orson Welles, Clifford Odets, and Arthur Miller. Actress Lee Grant was blacklisted for refusing to implicate her husband.

But many did name names, including Elia Kazan, who was called before the committee in January 1952. Kazan was born in Turkey and had come to America during the Depression. As a young man, when he belonged to the Group Theatre, Kazan had been a member of the Communist party, but later became disillusioned with their politics and renounced them. The committee wanted to know who else in the Group had attended meetings. At first, Kazan refused to answer, but after the president of Twentieth Century Fox studios threatened that Kazan would never work in Hollywood again, he contacted HUAC and identified eight former colleagues at the Group. News of his actions sent shockwaves through both the film and theater communities.

What particularly rankled many was that even if Kazan had been blacklisted in Hollywood, he would still have had his thriving theater career. Broadway did not have a blacklist because unlike Hollywood, which was under the control of a few powerful moguls who financed films, plays were financed and produced by any number of diverse people and companies.

Although others in the industry divulged names, Kazan became the poster child for betrayal, in part because of his defiant, unapologetic stance afterward. While Kazan continued to work in both film and theater, he was unwelcome in many circles within both industries. His one-time close friend, playwright Arthur Miller, who served jail time for rebuffing HUAC, didn't speak to Kazan for over a decade. Interestingly, though, Miller supported his receiving the Oscar for Lifetime Achievement.

Miller wrote in the *Guardian*, "My feelings toward that terrible era are unchanged, but at the same time history ought not to be rewritten. Elia Kazan did sufficient extraordinary work in theater and film to merit acknowledgement. . . . Perhaps all one can hope for is to find in one's heart praise for what a man has done well and censure for where he has tragically failed."[9]

Elia Kazan died on September 28, 2003, at his home in Manhattan.

For Your Information

After suffering a bout of writer's block during a separation from Frank Merlo, Williams began taking barbiturates. He would later admit that his drug use became an addiction, and he would struggle with it for the last two decades of his life. Although he never stopped writing, Williams's last important work was 1961's *Night of the Iguana*. He died February 24, 1983.

Chapter 10

Merciless Time

For all he had achieved, what obsessed and haunted Tennessee Williams was all he had squandered through the pursuit of loveless, anonymous sex as mindless diversion. He used this emotional anguish as the subtext for the brutally honest *Suddenly Last Summer*. Author Donald Spoto observed: "He wrote a play that wept for the waste—most of all because he felt that he had abused the freedom of the creative life, and of life itself. He had squandered what had been denied to his sister."[1]

The one-act play is stunning in its brutality. Violet Venable is trying to get her beautiful niece, Catharine, lobotomized to make sure she never reveals the truth about the death of her cousin Sebastian, Violet's son. The doctor she summons instead gives Catharine a truth serum and eventually learns the details about what happened so suddenly, last summer: Sebastian is a poet who writes one poem a summer. Because Violet has suffered a stroke, for the first time she will not be able to accompany him on his summer vacation, so Sebastian takes his cousin Catharine. She soon realizes he is using her to attract young men. When Sebastian loses focus and can't write, he begins to cruise the beach, where it is implied he exploits local street boys for sex. One day, a group of the boys surrounds Catharine and Sebastian. He tries to run away, but the children catch him and literally devour him, causing Catharine to go mad.

Spoto concludes, "Sebastian Venable's exploitation of others, his empty, decreative life and his abuse of his cousin Catharine were for Williams the clearest portrait he could draw of his own remorse. The play is, then, both confession and act of penance."[2]

Suddenly Last Summer was paired with another one-act, *Something Unspoken,* and opened off-Broadway at the York Theatre. To Williams's surprise, the play got rave reviews and enjoyed a successful run. Like so many of his other plays, *Suddenly Last Summer* was optioned by Hollywood for a film. In total, Williams would earn over $4 million for film versions of his plays, which in today's money would be worth over $26 million. However, because of his early years of struggle, Williams still worried about being broke—although by all accounts he was generous and always helped any friend in need.

The other play to evolve out of his therapy sessions was *Sweet Bird of Youth,* which deals with lost youth and lost innocence and the relentlessness of time passing. Again, there is stunning violence presented, which Williams would later say was probably gratuitous.

In the play, actress Alexandra Del Lago is trying to make a comeback fifteen years after retiring. When a preview audience reacts negatively to her new film, she runs away in a panic. She picks up a young man, Chance Wayne, who agrees to be her paid companion, and they take off together. Wayne, an aspiring actor, figures being with Alexandra is a smart career move.

The two stop in Wayne's hometown. He is hoping to rekindle a romance with his former childhood sweetheart, Heavenly Finley. He had originally left town seventeen years earlier after Heavenly's father, Boss Finley, decided Chance wasn't good enough for his daughter.

Chance now finds out that he had given Heavenly a venereal disease, which left her barren. When her still-irate father learns Chance is back, he warns him to leave immediately and stay away from Heavenly.

When Alexandra finds out her film is a huge success, she dumps Chance, who refuses to leave his hometown. He persists in trying to win back Heavenly's heart but fails. In retaliation for what he did to her, Boss Finley has Chance castrated. (In the movie version, he instead has his face slashed.)

Reviewers' reactions ranged from disappointment to frustration to anger at what many considered nothing more than shock tactics. Academics agreed. In the *Tulane Drama Review*, Henry Popkin wrote, "Williams now seems to be in a sort of race with himself . . . as if he is trying to see how far he can push the Gothic mode of playwriting."[3]

Interestingly, though, when the play opened at the Martin Beck Theatre on March 10, 1959, the audience responded enthusiastically. *Sweet Bird of Youth* would have a ten-month run and be another financial success, but Williams felt little cheer, only panic as he slipped steadily into drug and alcohol dependency.

Over the next four years his relationship with Merlo slowly but steadily slipped away. Williams's paranoia sharpened, and he began to separate himself from longtime friends and associates. In 1961, he moved to a new producer for *Night of the Iguana,* bypassing Cheryl Crawford, who had produced more of his plays than anyone. The slight was the first step in pushing her out of his life.

In an essay written for *Esquire*, Williams tossed barbs at his agent of twenty years, Audrey Wood, in essence accusing her of being an overbearing mother figure. It was a shockingly ungracious portrait of the woman who had been his staunchest supporter and who had literally kept him off the street as a struggling writer. With customary grace, Wood never confronted Williams, although she sensed their association was probably coming to a close. It did in 1971, after one of Williams's irrational emotional outbursts.

Night of the Iguana, about a defrocked minister looking for spiritual and personal redemption, premiered December 28, 1961, at the Royale Theatre. Another success, the show ran for 316 performances before closing the following September. It earned the playwright his fourth Drama Critics' Circle Award. It would be Tennessee Williams's last important theatrical work.

In the summer of 1962, Williams received an urgent telegram from Audrey Wood. Friends of Merlo in Key West had contacted her—Frank was seriously ill. Tennessee dropped everything and was at Frank's bedside the next day. Originally, doctors diagnosed him with bronchial pneumonia . . . or maybe mononucleosis. After several months it became clear that Merlo was getting sicker. He came to New York for tests and the news was grim. A lifelong three-pack-a-day smoker, Merlo had inoperable lung cancer. He was dying.

Williams's friend Meade Roberts recalled to Donald Spoto, "As Frank became more and more ill, Tennessee certainly realized how wrong he'd been about his life with Frank, how unfair and how selfish and ungiving to Frank he'd been in the last few years."[4]

Williams tried to be more attentive, but Merlo spent much of his time alone in his room, leaving Williams to fend for himself—something he was not equipped to do.

Frank Corsaro, who directed *Night of the Iguana*, observed, "By this time, Tennessee had come to believe in his failures even more than his successes. The failures . . . were tangible and provable, and the successes he tended to think of as . . . accidents that could never be repeated. He was incapable of relying on himself or his own strengths and I think that is why he turned to those bereft souls who provided him with easy distraction and no challenges."[5]

Frank Merlo died in September 1963, sending Williams into a years-long depression mired in a haze of pills and alcohol. In 1969, he suffered a complete breakdown. His brother Dakin committed him to the psychiatric unit of the Barnes Hospital in St. Louis to be treated for his addictions.

A year later, on David Frost's talk show, Williams revealed to the public that he was gay. He also openly discussed his sexuality in his 1975 memoirs, which offered new insight to his work and how his childhood and relationship with his family informed his writing.

As always, Williams kept writing but was never able to recapture the magic. He acknowledged to the *New York Times*, "I'm very conscious of my decline in popularity but I don't permit it to stop me because I have the example of so many playwrights before me. . . . And to me it has been providential to be an artist, a great act of providence that I was able to turn my borderline psychosis into creativity—my sister Rose did not manage this. So I keep writing. I am sometimes pleased with what I do—for me, that's enough."[6]

But Williams knew the clock was ticking. "It haunts me, the passage of time," he admitted to Robert Rice. "I think time is a merciless thing. I think life is a process of burning oneself out and time is the fire that burns you. But I think the spirit of man is a good adversary."[7]

In a letter to Molly Day Thacher, Williams once boasted, "My whole life has been a series of escapes, physical or psychological, more miraculous than any Houdini."[8] On a cold winter night, he finally ran out of miracles.

On Friday, February 24, 1983, Tennessee Williams was found dead at the Hotel Elysée on East Fifty-fourth Street in New York. His body was discovered at 10:45 A.M. by his secretary John Uecker, who shared the suite with Williams.

New York City's chief medical examiner, Dr. Elliot Gross, determined Williams had choked on a plastic cap. It is believed that after a night of heavy drinking and recreational drug use, Williams used the cap as a makeshift pill cup to take his nightly barbiturates. While downing the pills, the cap accidentally lodged in his throat. He was apparently too stoned for his gag reflex to kick in.

As news of his death circulated, a flood of tributes followed, honoring his creative legacy. Those who knew him best mourned the man and his foibles.

"Yes, he certainly wasn't happy," Lady St. Just told the *New York Times*. "But there was this wonderful thing he once said. . . . A reporter asked him, 'What is your definition of happiness, Mr. Williams?' And Tennessee answered, 'Insensitivity, I guess.'

"That was Tennessee. He wasn't particularly good looking. He was clumsy: You couldn't put him in a limousine, because he'd fall out the other side. If there was something to trip over, the darling would trip over it. But there was his genius. He had X-ray eyes, and they went right into situations. He felt so deeply about everything. He was just so passionate, and he understood the smallest detail that would be in anybody's heart, the tiniest desire, the tiniest rejection, the tiniest affection. He would just sense it."[9]

The notion that great art can only come from great pain may seem like a cliché, but in the case of Tennessee Williams it happened to be true. His lifelong struggle with the dark side of his nature infused and informed his work with an emotionally raw voice that is at once soulful and profane and forever changed the possibilities of what a play could be. It is also that deeply imbedded humanity that keeps his work relevant decades after his death and will continue to resonate with each new generation.

Despite his stated preference to be buried at sea where Hart Crane had jumped overboard, Thomas Lanier Williams was laid to rest at Calvary Cemetery in St. Louis, next to his mother.

Key West

Tennessee Williams spent much of his adult life traveling, living out of hotels or taking short-term leases. The only place he ever bought a house was in Key West, Florida, the southernmost city in the continental United States. Since its founding, the tiny island has had a unique appeal for artists of all kinds.

The Florida Keys—*key* is another word for "low island"—were discovered by Ponce de Leon in 1513. At the time, southern Florida was the home of the Calusa Indians, who were skilled fishers and sailors. As more European settlers came to the New World, indigenous Indian tribes on the east coast kept getting pushed farther south.

Eventually, the Calusa's territory was invaded by displaced tribes from Georgia and South Carolina. In the fighting that followed, many of the Calusa were captured and sold as slaves. Many other Calusa died from diseases, such as smallpox, brought to Florida by European explorers. It is believed the small number of remaining Calusa sailed to Cuba in the late eighteenth century, when Florida became a British colony, although no information on what happened to them after can be found.

According to legend, when the first explorers landed on Key West, they found the beach covered with bones—remains from one of the battles the Calusa fought with invading tribes. As a result, the island was originally called *Cayo Hueso*, or Bone Key.

Control of the keys switched back and forth between Spain and Britain until 1819 when Florida became a United States possession. That didn't stop Cubans and other Caribbeans from sailing to the Keys to fish, salvage shipwrecks, and cut down the plentiful hardwood trees. By this time *Cayo Hueso* was called Key West, believed to be an Anglicized distortion of its Spanish name.

Its location and natural deep harbor prompted the U.S. Navy to establish Key West as an official U.S. port of entry in 1822. However, the nearby reefs were treacherous and the weather unpredictable, so many ships ended up wrecking on their way into Key West. After any wreck, the local citizens would salvage the ships, and many got rich as a result. From 1828 to the early 1850s, Key West was the wealthiest city, based on population, in the United States. It also remained the most isolated. Railroad baron Henry Flagler decided to build the Over-Sea Railroad, which was completed in 1912, connecting Key West to the mainland.

After Prohibition was passed, the Florida Keys became entryways for rum and other liquor smuggled into the country from Cuba and the

Caribbean islands. Then Key West, like the rest of the country, was hard hit during the Great Depression, and the city declared bankruptcy.

In 1935, the Over-Sea Railroad was destroyed during a hurricane and in the 1980s was replaced with the Over-Sea Highway. Known as US 1, it is 126 miles long, with more than forty bridges connecting the Keys to the coast of Florida. Once the highway was completed, tourism became Key West's biggest business. Among those drawn to the island was John James Audubon, who spent time on the island painting the local bird life.

Over-Sea Railroad

Tennessee Williams first traveled to Key West in the early 1940s and eventually bought a house there in 1947. Up to his death, he listed his Key West home as his permanent address. Meanwhile, the island's most famous resident was author Ernest Hemingway. According to lore, Hemingway wrote the final draft of *A Farewell to Arms* and the short stories *The Snows of Kilimanjaro* and *The Short Happy Life of Francis Macomber* while staying at his Key West home, which had been a wedding present from his wife's wealthy uncle. He also set his novel *To Have and Have Not* in Key West during its bleak Great Depression days.

Perhaps the most curious incident in the island's history came on April 23, 1982, when Key West and the other Keys briefly declared their independence from the United States and named their new sovereignty the Conch Republic. The action was to protest a blockade by the U.S. Border Patrol to prevent Cuban refugees from entering the country. It wasn't that the people of the Keys were defending the refugees who were seeking a better life. Rather, when the Border Patrol searched cars, it blocked the Over-Sea Highway, putting a crimp in Key West's tourism. Although the "secession" lasted only a day, the establishment of the Conch Republic is remembered by Keys residents during an annual weeklong Independence celebration every April.

Chronology

1909 Older sister, Rose, is born, who will later be the inspiration for Laura in *The Glass Menagerie*

1911 Thomas Lanier Williams is born on March 26 in Columbus, Mississippi

1918 The Williams family moves to St. Louis

1927 Places third in a national essay writing contest

1938 Graduates from the University of Iowa

1939 Moves to New Orleans and begins writing as "Tennessee" Williams, his college nickname

1943 Is hired as a writer by MGM Studios

1945 *The Glass Menagerie* opens on Broadway and wins New York Drama Critics' Circle Award

1947 Meets Frank Merlo, who becomes his life partner; wins the Pulitzer Prize for *A Streetcar Named Desire*

1951 *The Rose Tattoo* wins the Tony for Best Drama

1955 Wins his second Pulitzer for *Cat on a Hot Tin Roof*

1957 Tennessee's father, Cornelius "C.C." Williams, dies

1958 *Suddenly Last Summer* begins a successful Broadway run

1963 Frank Merlo dies of lung cancer, sending Williams further into depression and drug use

1969 Is institutionalized for drug dependency

1970 Publicly acknowledges his homosexuality on *The David Frost Show*

1975 Receives Medal of Honor for Literature from National Arts Club; publishes *Memoirs*

1980 His mother, Edwina Williams, dies

1983 Chokes to death on a bottle cap at the Hotel Elysée in New York on February 24

1995 US Postal Service issues a Tennessee Williams stamp

1996 Rose dies September 4 at age eighty-seven

Selected Works

The Glass Menagerie

27 Wagons Full of Cotton, and Other One Act Plays

A Streetcar Named Desire

Summer and Smoke

The Rose Tattoo

Camino Real

Cat on a Hot Tin Roof

Orpheus Descending

Suddenly Last Summer

Sweet Bird of Youth

The Night of the Iguana

The Milk Train Doesn't Stop Here Anymore

Vieux Carré

Timeline in History

1868 Louisa May Alcott writes *Little Women*.

1910 William Sydney Porter, better known as O. Henry, dies.

1920 The first commercial radio station begins broadcasting.

1921 James Joyce's *Ulysses* is labeled as obscene material in the U.S.

1925 Harold Ross founds *The New Yorker* magazine.

1927 Hollywood produces the first talking picture, *The Jazz Singer*.

1930 Television broadcasting begins.

1940 John Steinbeck wins Pulitzer Prize for *The Grapes of Wrath*.

1948 Jack Kerouac is credited for coining the term *beat generation*.

1953 Lawrence Ferlinghetti and Peter Martin open the City Lights Bookstore in San Francisco.

1954 Ernest Hemingway wins Nobel Prize for Literature.

1958 *San Francisco Chronicle* columnist Herb Caen coins the term *beatnik*.

1963 Betty Friedan's *The Feminine Mystique* spurs the women's movement.

1964 The Supreme Court rules that Henry Miller's *Tropic of Cancer* is not obscene and that any work of literary merit may not be labeled as such.

1974 President Nixon is forced to resign after an investigation of a break-in at the Democratic National Committee headquarters by reporters Carl Bernstein and Bob Woodward eventually leads to a congressional inquiry.

1989 Iran's Ayatollah Khomeini offers a $1 million reward to any Muslin who kills writer Salman Rushdie for writing the book *Satanic Verses*.

1992 The number of U.S. newspapers offering news online increases to 150.

1996 Oprah Winfrey gives publishing a huge boost in sales with her talk show's monthly book club.

2005 The *Harry Potter* book series surpasses 300 million books sold worldwide.

2006 State and federal governments debate whether to ban gay marriages or make them legal.

Chapter Notes

Chapter 1
An Overnight Success

1. Tennessee Williams, *The Glass Menagerie* (New York: New Directions, 1999).

2. Tennessee Williams, *Memoirs* (Garden City, New York: Doubleday & Company, 1972), p. 81.

3. Donald Spoto, *The Kindness of Strangers: The Life of Tennessee Williams* (Boston: Little, Brown & Company, 1985), p. 110.

4. Ibid.

5. Spoto, p. 111.

6. Williams, *Memoirs,* p. 85.

7. Claudia Cassidy, "Fragile Drama Holds Theatre in Tight Spell," *Chicago Daily Tribune*, December 27, 1944, p. 11.

8. Donald Spoto, "Laurette Taylor in *The Glass Menagerie,*" 1985, http://www.eiu.edu/~eng1002/authors/williams5/Laurette.htm

9. Williams, *Memoirs,* p. 85.

10. Claudia Cassidy, "On the Aisle," *Chicago Daily Tribune*, January 7, 1945, p. E3.

11. Claudia Cassidy, "On the Aisle," *Chicago Daily Tribune*, January 18, 1945, p. 16.

12. Spoto, *The Kindness of Strangers,* p. 111.

13. Williams, *Memoirs*, p. 84.

14. Mel Gussow, "Tennessee Williams Is Dead at 71," *New York Times*, February 26, 1983, http://partners.nytimes.com/books/00/12/31/specials/williams-obit.html

15. Spoto, *The Kindness of Strangers,* pp. 116–117.

16. Ibid., p. 110.

17. Tennessee Williams, "Creator of *The Glass Menagerie* Pays Tribute to Laurette Taylor," *New York Times,* December 5, 1949, http://www.nytimes.com/books/00/12/31/specials/williams-taylor.html

18. Ibid.

Chapter 2
The Outcasts

1. Edwina Dakin Williams and Lucy Freeman, *Remember Me to Tom* (New York: G.P. Putnam's Sons, 1963), pp. 23–24.

2. Donald Spoto, *The Kindness of Strangers: The Life of Tennessee Williams* (Boston: Little, Brown & Company, 1985), p. 11.

3. Lyle Leverich, *Tom: The Unknown Tennessee Williams* (New York: Crown, 1995), p. 49.

4. Williams and Freeman, pp. 20–21.

5. Ibid., p. 19.

6. Ibid., p. 26.

7. Tennessee Williams, *Memoirs* (Garden City, New York: Doubleday & Company, 1972), p. 13.

8. Lyric Opera San Diego, "*The Mikado:* Gilbert and Sullivan, the Collaborators," http://www.lyricoperasandiego.com/Education/PeopleGS.htm

Chapter 3
A Difficult Transition

1. Edwina Dakin Williams and Lucy Freeman, *Remember Me to Tom* (New York: G.P. Putnam's Sons, 1963), p. 28.

2. Tennessee Williams, *Memoirs* (Garden City, New York: Doubleday & Company, 1972), p. 13.

3. Donald Spoto, *The Kindness of Strangers: The Life of Tennessee Williams* (Boston: Little, Brown & Company, 1985), p. 16.

4. Phone Interview with Dakin Williams by Don'dria Moore, 2000, http://www.shs.starkville.k12.ms.us/mswm/MSWritersAndMusicians/writers/TennesseeWilliams/tennesseewilliams2.html

5. Williams, *Memoirs,* pp. 13–14.

6. Williams and Freeman, p. 32.

7. Spoto, p. 20.

8. Williams and Freeman, p. 57.

9. Ibid.

10. Spoto, p. 19.

11. Lyle Leverich, *Tom: The Unknown Tennessee Williams* (New York: Crown, 1995), p. 192.

Chapter 4
Season in Hell

1. Edwina Dakin Williams and Lucy Freeman, *Remember Me to Tom* (New York: G.P. Putnam's Sons, 1963), p. 51.

2. Mel Gussow, "Tennessee Williams on Art and Sex," *New York Times*, November 3, 1975, http://partners.nytimes.com/books/00/12/31/specials/williams-art.html

3. Donald Spoto, *The Kindness of Strangers: The Life of Tennessee Williams* (Boston: Little, Brown & Company, 1985), p. 35.

4. Ibid., p. 37.

5. Williams and Freeman, p. 65.

6. Spoto, p. 51.

7. Ibid.

8. Robert Rice, "A Man Named Tennessee," *New York Post*, April 28, 1958, p. M-2.

9. Henry Schvey, "Examining Tennessee Williams's University Blues," *Washington University in St. Louis Magazine*, Summer 2005, http://magazine.wustl.edu/Summer05/Viewpoint.htm

10. Ibid.

11. Ibid.

Chapter 5
On the Road

1. John Calendo, "Tennessee Talks to John Calendo," *Interview*, April 1973.

2. Tennessee Williams, *Memoirs* (Garden City, New York: Doubleday & Company, 1972), p. 47.

3. Edwina Dakin Williams and Lucy Freeman, *Remember Me to Tom* (New York: G.P. Putnam's Sons, 1963), p. 85.

4. Ibid., p. 84.

5. Ibid., p. 85.

6. Tom Buckley, "Tennessee Williams Survives," *The Atlantic*, November 1970.

7. Robert Berkvist, "An Interview With Tennessee Williams," *New York Times*, December 21, 1975, http://partners.nytimes.com/ books/00/12/31/specials/ williams-interview75.html

8. Williams and Freeman, pp. 85–86.

9. Williams, p. 47.

10. Gilbert Maxwell, *Tennessee Williams and Friends* (Cleveland: World Publishing Company, 1965), p. 256.

11. Williams, p. 49.

12. Ibid.

13. Williams and Freeman, p. 97.

14. Donald Spoto, *The Kindness of Strangers: The Life of Tennessee Williams* (Boston: Little, Brown & Company, 1985), p. 67.

15. Tennessee Williams, "A Writer's Quest for a Parnassus," *New York Times*, August 13, 1950, http://partners.nytimes.com/books/ 00/12/31/specials/williams-parnassus. html

16. Mel Gussow, "Tennessee Williams on Art and Sex," *New York Times*, November 3, 1975, http://partners.nytimes.com/books/ 00/12/31/specials/williams-art.html

17. Williams, p. 51.

18. Williams and Freeman, p. 105.

19. Ibid., p. 106.

Chapter 6
Breakthrough

1. Audrey Wood, with Max Wilk, *Represented by Audrey Wood* (New York: Doubleday, 1981), p. 133.

2. Edwina Dakin Williams and Lucy Freeman, *Remember Me to Tom* (New York: G.P. Putnam's Sons, 1963), p. 112.

3. Ibid., p. 110.

4. Donald Spoto, *The Kindness of Strangers: The Life of Tennessee Williams* (Boston: Little, Brown & Company, 1985), p. 79.

5. Ibid., p. 80.

6. Alexander Williams, untitled article, *The Boston Herald*, December 31, 1940, p. 10.

7. Williams and Freeman, p. 113.

8. Ibid., p. 143.

9. Harold Bloom, editor, *Tennessee Williams's the Glass Menagerie*, Contributors (New York: Chelsea House, 1988), p. 4.

10. Williams and Freeman, p. 153.

11. Bruce Smith, *Costly Performances* (New York: Paragon House, 1990) p. 6.

Chapter 7
Brutal Desire

1. Francis Donahue, *The Dramatic World of Tennessee Williams* (New York: Ungar, 1964), p. 29.

2. "The Angel of the Odd," *Time*, March 9, 1962, http://www.time.com/time/magazine/article/0,9171,939962,00.html

3. Christine Day and Bob Woods, editors, *Where I Live: Selected Essays by Tennessee Williams* (New York: New Directions, 1978) p. 72.

4. Harold Bloom, editor, *Tennessee Williams's a Streetcar Named Desire*, Contributors (New York: Chelsea House. 1988), p. 99.

5. Ibid., p. 54.

6. Ibid., p. 67.

7. Tennessee Williams, *Memoirs* (Garden City, New York: Doubleday & Company, 1972), p. 131.

8. Donald Spoto, *The Kindness of Strangers: The Life of Tennessee Williams* (Boston: Little, Brown & Company, 1985), p. 135.

9. T. Cole and H. Chinoy, editors, *Directing the Play* (New York, Bobbs-Merrill, 1953), p. 42.

10. LitWeb.net, *Tennessee Williams* http://www.biblion.com/litweb/biogs/williams_tennessee.html

11. Ann B. Tracy, *The Gothic Novel 1790–1830 Plot Summaries and Index to Motifs* (Lexington: University Press of Kentucky, 1981), http://www.usask.ca/english/frank/gothtrad.htm

12. Edwina Dakin Williams and Lucy Freeman, *Remember Me to Tom* (New York: G.P. Putnam's Sons, 1963), p. 213.

Chapter 8
"The Little Horse"

1. Maria St. Just, *Five O'Clock Angel: Letters of Tennessee Williams to Maria St. Just* (New York: Knopf, 1990), p. 3.

2. Donald Spoto, *The Kindness of Strangers: The Life of Tennessee Williams* (Boston: Little, Brown & Company, 1985), p. 150.

3. Tennessee Williams, *Memoirs* (Garden City, New York: Doubleday & Company, 1972), p. 156.

4. Spoto, p. 153.

5. Ibid.

6. Edwina Dakin Williams and Lucy Freeman, *Remember Me to Tom* (New York: G.P. Putnam's Sons, 1963), p. 200.

7. Spoto, p. 160.

8. Ibid., p. 172.

9. Stephanie Sheh, "Sexual Nuances, Complexity of 'The Rose Tattoo' Make for Rare Treat," UCLA *Daily Bruin*, Thursday, October, 17, 1996.

10. Janet Montefiore, *Men and Women Writers of the 1930s: The Dangerous Flood of History* (New York: Routledge, 1996), p. 50.

11. Robert Liddell, *A Treatise on the Novel* (London: J. Cape, 1947), p. 33.

Chapter 9
Mendacity

1. Donald Windham, *Footnotes to a Friendship* (Verona: Stamperia Valdonega, 1983), p. 262.

2. *The Internet Theater Magazine of Reviews,* Features, Annotated Listings, *Camino Real* http://www.curtainup.com/caminoreal.html

3. Donald Spoto, *The Kindness of Strangers: The Life of Tennessee Williams* (Boston: Little, Brown & Company, 1985), p. 187.

4. CurtainUp, *Camino Real, A CurtainUp Berkshire Review,* http://www.curtainup.com/caminoreal.html

5. PBS, Online NewsHour, November 11, 1997, http://www.pbs.org/newshour/bb/entertainment/july-dec97/streetcar_11-11.html

6. Bruce Smith, *Costly Performances* (New York: Paragon House, 1990), p. 17.

7. Edwina Dakin Williams and Lucy Freeman, *Remember Me to Tom* (New York: G.P. Putnam's Sons, 1963), p. 202.

8. Robert Rice, "A Man Named Tennessee," *New York Post*, April 28, 1958, p. M-2.

9. Arthur Miller, "Why Elia Should Get His Oscar," *Guardian*, March 6, 1999 http://film.guardian.co.uk/The_Oscars_1999/Story/0,,36079,00.html

Chapter 10
Merciless Time

1. Donald Spoto, *The Kindness of Strangers: The Life of Tennessee Williams* (Boston: Little, Brown & Company, 1985), p. 223.

2. Ibid.

3. Henry Popkin, "The Plays of Tennessee Williams," *Tulane Drama Review*, March, 1960, p. 64.

4. Spoto, p. 257.

5. Ibid.

6. Michiko Kakutani, "Tennessee Williams: 'I Keep Writing. Sometimes I Am Pleased,'" *New York Times*, August 13, 1981, http://partners.

nytimes.com/books/00/12/31/specials/
williams-obit.html

7. Robert Rice, "A Man Named Tennessee," *New York Post*, April 28, 1958, p. M-2.

8. Upjournals.com, review. Albert J. Devlin and Nancy M. Tischler, editors, *The Selected Letters of Tennessee Williams*, vol. I, 1920–1945 (New York: New Directions, 2000), http://www.

utpjournals.com/product/utq/712/712_review_parker.html

9. Mervyn Rothstein, "Remembering Tennessee Williams as a Gentle Genius of Empathy," *New York Times*, May 30, 1990, http://partners. nytimes.com/books/00/12/31/specials/williams-empathy.html

Further Reading

For Young Adults

Heintzelman, Greta, and Alycia Smith-Howard. *Critical Companion to Tennessee Williams*. New York: Facts on File, 2005.

McCullers, Carson. *The Heart Is a Lonely Hunter*. New York: Modern Library. Reissue edition, 1993.

Nelson, Bejamin. *The Major Plays of Tennessee Williams: Cat on a Hot Tin Roof/The Glass Menagerie/Orpheus Descending/A Streetcar Named Desire and Others*. Brentwood, TN: Monarch Press, 1985.

Works Consulted

Bloom, Harold, editor. *Tennessee Williams's The Glass Menagerie*. Contributors. New York: Chelsea House, 1988.

———. *Tennessee Williams's A Streetcar Named Desire*. Contributors. New York: Chelsea House, 1988.

Cole, T., and H. Chinoy, editors. *Directing the Play*. New York, Bobbs-Merrill, 1953.

Crandall, George W. *The Critical Response to Tennessee Williams*. Westport, CT: Greenwood Press, 1996.

Day, Christine, and Bob Woods, editors. *Where I Live: Selected Essays by Tennessee Williams*. New York: New Directions, 1978.

Devlin, Albert J. *Conversations with Tennessee Williams*. University Press of Mississippi, 1985.

Devlin, Albert J., and Nancy M. Tischler, editors. *The Selected Letters of Tennessee Williams*, vol. I, 1920–1945. New York: New Directions, 2000.

Donahue, Francis. *The Dramatic World of Tennessee Williams*. New York: Ungar, 1964.

Kazan, Elia. *A Life*. New York; Knopf, 1988.

Leverich, Lyle. *Tom: The Unknown Tennessee Williams*. New York: Crown, 1995.

Liddell, Robert. *A Treatise on the Novel*. London: J. Cape, 1947.

Maxwell, Gilbert. *Tennessee Williams and Friends*. Cleveland: World Publishing Company, 1965.

Popkin, Henry. "The Plays of Tennessee Williams." *Tulane Drama Review*, March 1960.

St. Just, Maria. *Five O'Clock Angel: Letters of Tennessee Williams to Maria St. Just*. New York: Knopf, 1990.

Smith, Bruce. *Costly Performances*. New York: Paragon House, 1990.

Spoto, Donald. *The Kindness of Strangers: The Life of Tennessee Williams*. Boston: Little, Brown & Company, 1985.

Williams, Edwina Dakin, and Lucy Freeman, editor. *Remember Me to Tom*. New York: G.P. Putnam's Sons, 1963.

Williams, Tennessee. *Camino Real*. Norfolk: New Directions, 1953.

———. *The Glass Menagerie*. New York: New Directions, 1999.

———. *Memoirs*. Garden City, New York: Doubleday & Company, 1972.

———. *A Streetcar Named Desire*. New York: New Directions, 1947.

Windham, Donald. *Footnotes to a Friendship*. Verona, Italy: Stamperia Valdonega, 1983.

Wood, Audrey, with Max Wilk. *Represented by Audrey Wood*. New York: Doubleday, 1981.

Articles

"The Angel of the Odd." *Time*, March 9, 1962.

Berkvist, Robert. "An Interview with Tennessee Williams." *New York Times*, December 21, 1975.

Buckley, Tom. "Tennessee Williams Survives." *The Atlantic*, November 1970.

Buncombe, Andrew. "Poem by Troubled Tennessee Williams Found on Exam Pad." *The Independent*, April 2005. http://www.findarticles.com/p/articles/mi_qn4158/is_200504/ai_n13615424

Calendo, John. "Tennessee Talks to John Calendo." *Interview*, April 1973.

Cassidy, Claudia. "Fragile Drama Holds Theatre in Tight Spell." *Chicago Daily Tribune*, December 27, 1944.

———. "On the Aisle." *Chicago Daily Tribune*, January 7, 1945, p. E3.

———. "On the Aisle." *Chicago Daily Tribune*, January 18, 1945, p. 16.

Gardner, Elysa. "Tennessee Williams Is Hotter Than Ever." *USA Today*, October 21, 2003.

Gussow, Mel. "Tennessee Williams on Art and Sex." *New York Times,* November 3, 1975.

Kakutani, Michiko. "Tennessee Williams: 'I Keep Writing. Sometimes I Am Pleased.'" *New York Times*, August 13, 1981.

Rice, Robert. "A Man Named Tennessee." *New York Post*, April 28, 1958.

Rothstein, Mervyn. "Remembering Tennessee Williams as a Gentle Genius of Empathy." *New York Times*, May 30, 1990.

Schvey, Henry. "Examining Tennessee Williams's University Blues." *Washington University in St. Louis Magazine,* Summer 2005.

Sheh, Stephanie. "Sexual Nuances, Complexity of 'The Rose Tattoo' Make for Rare Treat." UCLA *Daily Bruin*, Thursday, October, 17, 1996.

Williams, Alexander. "Battle of Angels" review. *The Boston Herald*, December 31, 1940.

Williams, Tennessee. "A Writer's Quest for a Parnassus." *New York Times*, August 13, 1950.

———. "Creator of *The Glass Menagerie* Pays Tribute to Laurette Taylor," *New York Times,* December 5, 1949.

On the Internet

CurtainUp, Camino Real, A CurtainUp Berkshire Review
    http://www.curtainup.com/caminoreal.html

Gilbert & Sullivan Archive
    http://math.boisestate.edu/gas/

The Internet Theater Magazine of Reviews, Features, Annotated Listings, *Camino Real*
    http://www.curtainup.com/caminoreal.html

The John F. Kennedy Center, "Biography of Tennessee Williams"
    http://www.kennedy-center.org/calendar/index.cfm?fuseaction=
    showIndividual&entitY_id=3819&source_type=A

LitWeb.net, *Tennessee Williams*
    http://www.biblion.com/litweb/biogs/williams_tennessee.html

Lyric Opera San Diego, "*The Mikado:* Gilbert and Sullivan, the Collaborators"
    http://www.lyricoperasandiego.com/Education/PeopleGS.htm

Mississippi Writers and Musicians Project of Starkville High School
    http://www.shs.starkville.k12.ms.us/mswm/MSWritersAndMusicians/writers/
    TennesseeWilliams/tennesseewilliams2.html

Modern American Poetry
    http://www.english.uiuc.edu/maps/poets/a_f/crane/crane.htm

PBS, *American Masters: Tennessee Williams*
    http://www.pbs.org/wnet/americanmasters/database/williams_t.html

PBS, *Online NewsHour*, November 11, 1997
    http://www.pbs.org/newshour/bb/entertainment/july-dec97/
    streetcar_11-11.html

The Phineas Gage Information Page. Maintained by School of Psychology, Deakin
    University, Victoria, Australia
    http://www.deakin.edu.au/hmnbs/psychology/gagepage

Glossary

avant-garde (aa-vunt-GARD) experimental; daring.

antagonist (an-TAA-guh-nist) an adversary; a secondary character who provokes the main character into action.

barbiturate (bar-BIH-chuh-ret) a drug that depresses the central nervous system.

climax (KLY-maks) the decisive moment of a play or movie.

colloquial (kuh-LOH-kwee-ul) informal language, either spoken or written.

denouement (day-noo-MAH) the final resolution of a plot.

epigram (EH-puh-gram) a short, witty thought or observation.

exposition (ek-spuh-ZHIH-shun) in a play, dialogue that gives background information.

genre (ZHAWN-ruh) the style or type of a creative work.

gentility (jen-TIH-leh-tee) a high social status; elegance.

homosexuality (hoh-muh-sek-shuh-WAA-luh-tee) sexual attraction to someone who is of one's same gender.

inebriation (ih-nee-bree-AY-shun) the state of being drunk.

innuendo (in-yoo-EN-doh) an insinuation or subtle suggestion.

insuperable (in-SOO-pur-uh-bul) unable to be overcome.

libido (luh-BEE-doh) sex drive; sexual desire.

menagerie (meh-NAA-juh-ree) a collection of animals, often kept for exhibition.

mendacity (men-DAA-sih-tee) being deceitful; characterized by lies.

nonagenarian (NOH-nah-jen-NAYR-ee-an) someone who is 90 to 99 years old.

operetta (ah-per-EH-tah) a light opera with substantial spoken dialogue.

pathos (PAY-thohs) an emotion such as sympathy or pity.

plot (plaht) the events of a story.

protagonist (proh-TAH-guh-nist) the lead character in a play, movie, or novel.

pseudonym (SOO-doh-nim) a fictitious, or fake, name.

subtext (SUB-text) the unspoken meaning of what is being said.

surrogate (SIR-oh-get) a substitute or stand-in.

Index